THE ART OF

S~~MALL BUSINESS~~ S

ISBN: 0-75961-558-6

This book is printed on acid free paper.

1stbooks rev. 5/9/01

ACKNOWLEDGEMENT

I dedicate this book

to my

Devoted Wife Beverly

and

Wonderful Children

Linda, Larry, Howard and Lisa

Who tolerated and endured

my many years and long hours of business.

TABLE OF CONTENTS

ABOUT THE AUTHOR

Leon Albin was born and raised in modest surroundings. His father migrated from Romania in 1909, did menial jobs in Chicago until 1921, when he came to Baltimore and rented an abandoned German bakery to open a used clothing and World War I surplus store. Five children were raised on the second floor of this store, and Leon, the next to the youngest, was reared there until he was 17 years old.

After finishing high school, he entered the Navy at 18 and served almost two years until the end of World War II. He then entered the University of Baltimore while he worked three different jobs. In 1948 he got married, and in 1951 graduated from the University of Baltimore with a Bachelor of Science Degree in Marketing.

He worked in this little 2'x4' store (literally 12'x40') throughout college, and during the years from this humble beginning made many changes to merchandising. In 1953 he opened the second store, and with his father now retired, he was intent on building a chain of stores. The emphasis was now 100% on World War II surplus and related items, and he traded under the name of Lee's Surplus.

By 1968 our author, having operated stores throughout Maryland, changed his focus; this time on the outdoor field, specializing in camping, fishing, and hunting. This continued until 1980, with the name having been changed to Lee's Outdoor. The older locations were changed to stores more conducive to the merchandising trend.

Another transition and merchandising change occurred, and a new name -- Lee's Sports -- and motif emphasized athletic clothing, footwear and athletic gear. After building to seventeen stores in 1986, and at that time, the largest sporting goods chain in Maryland, Leon Albin sold out to a national chain.

Throughout these 38 years in business, he, like most small business people, had his ups and downs. Battling competition, merchandising, creditors, bankers, landlords, customers, employees, family sacrifices, etc.; it was a never-ending struggle to keep a successful venture going and to guard constantly against downfalls.

Selling out in 1986 was not a glamorous experience, because everybody wanted a piece of the action. In order to sell the core of the chain, he had to sell off or settle leases of the stores that were not in the desired market. Reducing the bank debts, selling off assets, settling with creditors, landlords, and keeping the morale of his employees high required ingenuity and perserverance.

His experience and knowledge is disclosed in this book to help others successfully confront the challenge of starting and managing a small business.

Following his business years, Leon Albin was elected to and served eight years in the Maryland House of Delegates. These two terms in office gave him further insight into dealing with small businesses. In the state legislature, he served on the Economic Matters Committee, and gained new perspectives on business, industry, and the economy.

A new career as a licensed realtor specializing in the commercial field, subsequently helped him to progress in the field of commerce.

The author lived a life punctuated with small business and people, and "The Art of Small Business Survival" puts into words the psychological fears of bankruptcy and failure, and the techniques of facing and solving these problems.

MY CAREER

I started my business career at eleven. My father had been operating a small antiquated store for fifteen years selling World War I surplus and used clothing. He had never updated any fixtures or advertising -- not even a sign in front of the store with a name.

One day he had a broken piece of pavement repaired. While the concrete was still wet, I carved my father's name on the pavement -- "Dave's Bargain Store" -- and thus started my "long and illustrious" career of advertising and promoting.

Then, while attending elementary through high school, I "floundered" around from job to job, serving newspapers, to being a Western Union delivery boy, to sweeping floors in a dry goods store, and other menial tasks "with no stability".

I proved to be a "floater" -- not having an earnest job. Then it happened at twenty-two. After serving in the U.S. Navy for almost two years during World War II, and while attending the University of Baltimore and holding down three jobs to support a new wife, I returned to my father's little used clothing store in 1948 for a serious career in business.

The years ahead toughened me up for all types of obstacles and successes that had to be dealt with on a regular basis. The key was to face the on-going situations that arose; be prepared, ready, and able to meet the confrontations and challenges; and take advantage of opportunities when they arose.

In 1953 our first transition occurred -- with a new store name -- Lee's Surplus, specializing in World War II surplus, catering to the working man. My father basically retired and our second location was opened.

Each year new stores were opened until 1968 when there were fifteen. At that time our image changed again to a rustic look and a new name -- Lee's Outdoor, specializing in the leisure field of camping, fishing, and hunting.

Slowly, we closed and re-opened locations to build another concept to the athletic field, and in 1980 again changed our image, our merchandising and our name to Lee's Sports, specializing in sporting goods, activewear and athletic shoes.

As a businessman for many years, I can attest to the successes and struggles during that period, and the many adaptations necessary to meet the changing times. Business decisions must be based on factors such as surroundings, needs, supply, demand, and competition.

While operating and building my stores, and after 28 years of business experience in conjunction with 25 years of active leadership in the community in which I resided, I thought it was time to give something back to my business community. By that time, five of my stores were located in different areas of Baltimore County. I saw the decaying and deterioration in the older areas, while new shopping centers were blossoming up all over.

I thought there was a need for a complete survey and evaluation of the fate and future of the stature and stability of these outdated areas of our county. I wrote a manual and analysis of this problem; contacted Theodore Venetoulis, County Executive of Baltimore County; and then met with him to discuss the plight. I pointed out the demand for a review and rehab of the business communities of Baltimore County, and the real void that existed in our county government in not having a rapport with small businesses. He then directed me to organize and appointed me as the first chairman of the Advisory Committee on Small Business for Baltimore County.

As such, we set up a 17-member committee from various types of businesses and localities with the main purpose of:

(1) Establishing a better understanding of the problems of small businesses in older areas;

(2) Adopting a progressive program to stimulate the sustenance of small business;

(3) Encouraging new investors;

(4)   Acting as liaison between Small Business and

Government.

Our mission was accomplished, as I feel our findings were a fore-runner to the establishment of the Revitalization Committee to rehab the older areas of Baltimore County.

My next step in politics was being elected to the Maryland State Central Democratic Committee, representing Baltimore County, which sets policy for the party.

After four years of service, I was appointed in 1982 to the Baltimore County Liquor Board as one of three commissioners governing and regulating approximately 750 businesses dealing in the sale and dispensing of alcoholic beverages. This gave me further insight into the problems of small businesses. Our board was responsible for controls, suspension, revocation, transferring, and granting of new licenses.

Understanding the shortcomings and oversights of inexperienced people with limited finances operating these establishments, illustrated to me that those coming up before our board should not always be burdened with stiff penalties. I was responsible for creating a rapport between our board and these businesses and, whenever practical, prescribing corrective measures rather than punitive damages.

1986 was the most pressured and stressful year of my life -- yet, in the end, the most accomplished. After transitions from used clothing, to surplus, to outdoor, and finally to sporting goods stores, my business was ripe once again for another step -- to being computerized. My stores had progressed as far as they could go with sound and recognizable merchandising, a well-accepted concept, image, and name. I had built a 17-store updated chain of the latest trends, equipment, athletic apparel, and shoes in diverse neighborhoods and shopping centers. Neither of my four children had interest to pursue the business; they each had different training and careers.

IT WAS TIME TO SELL OUT, and I thought I was ripe for a new career. This being the year for the Maryland State elections, I simultaneously sought to sell my business while filing for a seat in the House of Delegates (House of Representatives or Assemblymen in other states). The year of looking for a buyer while at the same time campaigning for public office proved to be quite an undertaking. My composure and patience was constantly being tested.

Selling my stores was a much bigger and broader project than I had anticipated. Through the years I had created a monster in different directions -- servicing unlike neighborhoods, both rural and urban areas, catering to various demographics, markets and people with a deviation of merchandise demands. Taking this apart turned out to be a meticulous and tedious chore.

My objective was exasperated because, despite many contacts and offerings, not one company had an interest in my diverse chain and absorbing the heavy debts that I had accumulated for expansions and inventory. This is always a pitfall of expanding small businesses. I needed to obliterate the large loan from the bank while wiping out the creditors' indebtedness. The only prospect of sale was being free and clear of inventory and debts -- an asset purchase, with the value placed on locations and leases.

My primary decision at this time was to sell off individual stores, settle certain undesirable leases and close and rent locations which I owned. This availed me the opportunity to absorb all the inventory with very little purchases while having sales to produce cash. I was then able to satisfy the bank and the many creditors while looking for a buyer for the desirable remaining portion of the prime locations.

During this time I was able to negotiate leases with Payless Shoe Source, the largest family shoe chain in the country, who had an interest to come into the Baltimore market. They were looking to open 175 stores in the Middle-Atlantic Market, and I was fortunate to supply them with their first four.

When I got down to the mall locations, Champs Sports (now owned by Woolworth) came into Baltimore environs and bought me out.

Now to politics and government: as I previously wrote, I was actively seeking a seat as a member of the Maryland House of Delegates. In early 1986 I was the fourth candidate to file for one of the three seats to represent approximately 100,000 people of our district. Before the filing deadline, however, in early July, there were 18 candidates. I was fortunate to win a four-year term and was re-elected in 1990 for a second four-year term.

In our legislative body, I quickly became known as a strong advocate for small business, and as a member of the House Economic Matters Committee helped set policy and regulated legislation and laws on insurance, business, and real estate. I sponsored and supported many bills dealing with issues in the above areas.

Among my most noteworthy concerns and interest was a result of my business days, wherein I had developed deep regard for stability and sustenance. I felt the need to focus in on programs for at-risk small businesses that required assistance to deal specifically with their economic problems in the area of guidance -- not only for refininancing, but more so to develop new technology, merchandising, and marketing, as well as management consulting.

Nearly every state in our country, including Maryland, have basic programs and emphasis in the areas of start-ups, funding partnerships, and encouraging business to the states -- but after much research, I was astounded to find out that there were no programs in any states on retention of faltering small businesses, helping for survival once they have operational and financial difficulties.

Strong efforts in this direction would not only boost our economy, but also salvage many tax dollars.

To fill this void, I worked with the Maryland Department of Economic Development to create new programs to identify and assist businesses at risk of failure to avert closures and maintain jobs.

Programs were ultimately developed to:

1. Refinance "at risk" businesses.

2. Consolidate operations and debt.

3. Marketing assistance.

4. New productive development.

5. Aid in new technology and merchandise.

6. Give counselling and guidance.

7. Plan implementation.

The above programs have been adopted by the Maryland Department of Economic Development as a fore-runner to those used by other states for similar needs for small businesses.

While my college days gave me the tools for the learning process, my 38 years in business was the real school of hard knocks. Dealing with the actual world of all the various phases of operations and merchandising can only be accomplished by participation and trial and error. Progress and success come with hard work and dedication, together with a strong goal orientation.

INTRODUCTION

Beating the threat of bankruptcy is an art few people have mastered. Holding on by a thread requires a strong backbone and a desire to achieve far-reaching expectations.

Business turnarounds are careful, meticulous and concentrated maneuvers which require changing of each activity. This creates an air of uneasiness that must rely on a sense of normality and calmness.

This book will focus on understanding yourself in this "hour" of crisis; how to remain composed and productive; to cope with both the routine and unusual trials and tribulations; and how to foresee creating new horizons in your venture based on innovative ideas and actions.

"The Art of Small Business Survival" is written to help retention of faltering small businesses and to promote a successful turnaround. This book discusses experiences faced by troubled enterprises and the psychological and bold methods used to overcome the fear and apprehension which leads to failure; also to improve the mental attitude for these crucial times.

You will further read about sound basic principles in facing financial setbacks and how to handle and enhance each function.

This book discusses facing the turnaround and maintaining and building a sound business.

"The Art of Small Business Survival" emphasizes the psychological approach for individuals to prepare for the difficult task of saving a troubled undertaking. Simplified procedures are introduced to help manage a company faced with bankruptcy.

Finally the book covers the more pleasant part of how to keep your operation intact, and suggestions for a brighter future.

Mending relationships and re-gaining confidence with bankers, creditors, suppliers, customers and employees is a very sigificant segment to the continuance of your company.

The chief executive officer of the turnaround operation, in addition to possessing knowledge, thorough understanding and skills, must demonstrate tenacity, vigor, conviction, toughness, exertion, commitment, the ability to make sensible decisions, and the listening attributes to hear suggestions, direction, and delegation of responsibilities.

He (or she) must move forward in a careful, yet deliberate approach to face the task ahead and must be mindful of the problems of the hazardous objective to reach the solutions to accomplish this mission.

Heavy aspirations and prompt action is necessary in order to make it apparent of the genuine effort to all interested and affected parties.

Methods in procedures must be sound; however decisions will not always be on target, but the dedication and resourcefulness and drive must continue.

A strong public relations of updating your revitalized business will go a long way toward future stability and progress. The feeling of satisfaction should be shared by everyone who played an integral part of its successful road to recovery. Displaying guts and perserverance, retaining their staying power, and keeping them involved for the future is a cherished goal. Everyone who shared the problem will want to be part of the solution. Anyone who became involved and who intermingled with this project of survival will benefit by the results.

Changing times, living conditions and needs are key factors in determining the operation of a successful adventure. Risks are directly related to the geographical, social and economical needs of your clientel, customers and consumers;

and supply and demand are factors to be considered very heavily.

Working toward an upward trend can be very painful, but the outlook of successful results will be very rewarding. Keep this in mind as an incentive to move ahead and don't let possible failure stand in your track. Always remember no setbacks will go away without your conscientious effort to make things happen.

It is my hope and intent in writing this book to help many troubled businesses find the road to recovery and the path to success. Many times advice and guidance avails to the entrepreneur the direction needed to turn a possible disaster into progress.

All the chapters in this book deal with subject matter which is directly and crucially related to the everyday operation of a business. You will review key factors and necessary steps in dealing with your usual activities; also where to turn and react to the burdensome daily chores.

Problems can become very threatening, but solutions will fall in place if you work at it. Looking ahead with the right attitude and the will to overcome can give you the opportunity to get things back on the right track. Pursuit, perserverance, staying composed and proper assistance will make the difference between success and failure. "The Art of Small Business Survival" covers the areas of a possible operations and financial disappointment to the opportunity for the retention of your faltering business.

CHAPTER 1

Business is a Dog-Eat-Dog Game

Prelude

The challenge of a business venture is a great vision, but one must not only be ready to reap the potential benefits, but be prepared to face pitfalls. Competition could be keen -- and trying -- but business is the survival of the fittest.

The world of small business is the Great American Dream for millions, who welcome the opportunity; ready to accept the challenge; and are prepared to react to changing times; with the skills and knowledge necessary for the tedious tasks ahead.

Operating a successful business is a composite of people working together within a common goal to aspire for an accomplished vision to reach an objective. In order to undertake and achieve the perpetuation and progress in building an ambitious project, strong merchandising and service must be emphasized.

Consumers are quick to form opinions and shape their shopping habits. Therefore, the development of your concept must show strength and direction. Strong consideration and thought must be given to be unique and distinctive. The end result is to be productive and profitable.

Regulating a business venture requires administering the necessary requisites on which to satisfy the demands and necessities to obtain acceptable and favorable achievements.

Being a good leader in business requires certain basic attributes and skills to be successful: You must be ready and willing to take risks -- although good judgment dictates when to be conservative.

Being innovative is a good characteristic to attract new customers, and upholding your convictions will affirm your beliefs. Always allow yourself to control your destiny by being involved as to what is happening. Everything is contingent on the three most important ingredients of suppliers, employees and customers.

Wouldn't it be wonderful if your aspirations and visions to risk going into a business were surely rewarded with success and growth? Well, unfortunately, it just doesn't happen that way. The majority of business opportunities fail in the first year -- and most others float up and down to "stay above water".

Economic recession is a cause for tough times -- one we cannot control. We can't correct the world around us or change conditions to improve our surroundings; however, we can build a "little" shell of circumstances that can be controlled through our every move and action.

Any business which gives the appearance of success and uniqueness automatically encourages others to simulate and copy its concept, location, products and merchandising techniques. So, in today's world of business there is only a small wonder for secrets or individuality of a venture to survive.

Competition and motivation for success creates the drive to stay one step ahead. Honesty and good ethics should prevail -- but beyond these fine virtues, a company must exert all efforts, energies and fortitude to show its supremacy and existence.

I had a competitor throughout the years who kept me on my toes. Both of us had stores throughout the state of Maryland -- have had one two doors apart -- and this became the battling grounds for taunting and provoking each other. He enjoyed doing everything he could to make me angry, try my patience, and test my skills. Likewise I became very arrogant and spiteful. We "had a ball" trying to run one another out of business.

One day he came up with the supreme competitive idea that was going to have me bow to his ingenuity by obliterating a line of merchandise which was similar and identifiable by our customers. It so happens that week both of our stores were promoting the exact items. Just as my window had large displays, so did his. The pricing was basically the same.

It is good business to know what your competition is doing and on a regular basis supervisors from both of our companies checked each other out. On this one occasion it was brought to his attention our likeness of promotion. Our competitor immediately cut one cent off of the entire list of approximately a dozen items. I then had my manager match his prices. The next day he again lowered prices by one cent, and I again matched everything. This went back and forth for about four days when I suddenly thought of the idea how to counteract this whole "game".

It so happened that his display windows were a flat front with only about a two foot indent at the door. In addition to our exterior windows, there was an indentation about fifteen feet from a long vestibule before the entrance. I then had my manager arrange for a very large exhibit in one of the side panels and cut every item twenty percent below cost. Then we put a large doubledecker bunk bed against the window display, covering almost all its visibility. Customers barely noticed anything with the blocked view -- but it didn't take one day before my competitor's supervisor was seen in the vestibule bending his head back and forth through the middle and on top of the bed noting all of our loss leaders and "killing" a very profitable line; no doubt, quite shattered and annoyed. Within two hours he was back after obviously reporting to his boss. He then ran into our store, cornered our manager saying "let's stop this stuff".

That was the end of all price wars on a direct basis. Of course, overall, we had to always check prices -- but never again did we ever have this type of intense cutting. In other words, in business you must keep up with your competition -- and even one step beyond.

Business competition can be a friendly battle; however, letting your guard down in the operation of your company can be devastating and costly in flourishing and even just maintaining your survival. You must constantly stay alert and have management and all those involved produce results of satisfaction and performance.

We have all seen how too often businesses that have taken off "flying high", expanding and growing at an unbelievable pace -- but then suddenly start a decline in an adverse direction. Many of these downfalls, if identified in a timely fashion, can be controlled and turned around back on an upward trend.

Sound and timely evaluation and a thorough study to determine the causes of the business decline must be started at the earliest detection. Outside consultants could be of utmost importance to play its part in this Dog-Eat-Dog game.

Every business has witnessed the experience of making the right decision at the appropriate time to sustain its upright balance as opposed to the improper approach to tilt the wrong way.

Throughout my years in business, my sustenance and growth was directly attributable to analyzing the market, making changes when necessary, maintaining a solid organization, good merchandising, keeping up with customers' needs, and always remaining cognizant of competition.

Survival is a constant battle and test for companies to maintain a regular design of character, profile, value, merchandise and assistance which appeal to the public. Nothing can deviate from these essential ingredients for existence.

Success and failure in small business is not a statistical crapshoot. Good management is the factor that determines survival and success. *Bad management is the factor that determines failure -- not the economy, the competition, the fickleness of customers, or bad luck. Bad management is responsible for over 90 percent of business failures.* About half of these failures are attributed to "incompetence" and the other half to "inadequate" prior experience.

Good management is the capacity to understand, direct and control the business and is based on an owner-manager's critical attentions to the few decisive factors of survival and success that make or break the business.

Supervision and directing a company requires certain basic principles of skill and habit:

- You must have a direction to pursue and build an organization which will carry out your purpose.
- Maintian methodical rules to follow.
- Sustain competent professionals and staff to maintain appropriate records and controls for direction.
- Produce or distribute desirable merchandise.
- Accumulate and have a cash surplus.

- Always have a handle on your business and a plan for the future.

A sound administration is more than the aggregate of the daily activities of the entrepreneur. It also comprises the attitudes, perceptions, thoughts, and knowledge -- the business acumen -- that motivate and govern crucial directorate activities.

Strategies That Worked in My Business

As a young, ambitious and apprehensive entrepreneur, I had great fears and trepidations about facing the real world of competition and "cut-throat".

I had the determination and guts to move into the task ahead, and was fully ready to approach the realistic risks of entering the business venture of my dreams.

I realized that if I were to be successful, I had to be prepared to generate my own path because no one was going to hand me a profitable business on a silver platter.

To compete against proven enterprises and to build a business to survive in the marketplace, I was ready and willing to work hard with long hours to cut the cost.

To swing the odds in my favor, I knew it was imperative that I put together a clear picture of how to proceed and act accordingly. A successful venture is no automatic result to a new beginning -- but is rather the commencement of a hard and tedious task.

I formulated in my mind and then a written design as to my plans, procedures and concept. I built up my enthusiasm, my convictions, and I was ready to go.

The point I am making is that I had the desire, and my goal was set to face the risks and problems to go into business, realizing it would not be easy to face the tough road ahead.

Leon Albin
Lessons Learned

- *Be objective. Self-delusion has no place in building a business. An honest, dispassionate assessment of the strengths and weaknesses of the company and your business and management skills is essential.*

- *Keep it simple and focused.*

- *Provide excellent and distinctive goods and services for your customers.*

- *Determine how to reach and sell your customers.*

- *Build, manage, and motivate a winning team.*

CHAPTER 2

The Hair-Line Between Success or Failure

Prelude

There is no room for too many errors in running a business. Each decision affects the entire operation, and crucial mistakes can make the difference between success or failure.

Upwards of 92% of all commerce in our country are small businesses and when people lose their jobs in industry and large corporations, they look to these ventures for their livelihoods. These enterprises are the backbone of this nation's economy for creating most of the jobs and prosperity. Our stability and growth depends on the success of the small business people.

What makes business such a unique career to pursue is the challenge, the opportunity and the unpredictability. Things can be going great, but sometimes a crucial decision on the wrong path can change an entire direction. Conversely, a right move can put the business "on top of the world" overnight. You can use the analogy of a boxing match between a smooth boxer and a slugger. The boxer was using a well-planned strategy, great foot action, dancing and jabbing the entire match, staying away from the slugger, accumulating points and winning the fight until the final round. Then, he got careless, went toe to toe with the slugger and it was all over with one punch.

Every day, each decision and all moves in business should be handled in a manner which affects the entire operation. The wrong plan could be costly and be the "straw that breaks the camel's back". On the other hand, companies can jump to a top position in their field with unusual creativity and taking quick advantage of the opportunity. Success in small business is heavily dependent on experience and your ability to make proper and timely judgments.

It is very distressful to see the numerous bankruptcies all around us each year. Many were old, well-known, successful and profitable companies for years, who were looked up to as the leaders in their field. Then a drastic and sudden change occurred that brought them down at a fast pace. In some cases, these businesses had a change in management, which followed a different trend that went sour. Others might have over-expanded at the wrong time; or over-extended their budgeting. Of course, the economy has a great affect on the ups and downs of business and industry. Those companies that do not follow the vital signs to blend in with changing conditions can become the unfortunate bearers.

Tough times can be a forerunner for the struggle ahead and can be a timely warning for tightening up your belt to re-evaluate your habits and prepare for the changes needed.

Ups and downs are common and normal in a business career -- but innate ability and drive can make the difference of adversity or prosperity. Good management is the key to success or failure.

Business could be thriving, having shown progress for years -- but a decline could happen almost suddenly. If you are watching your operation, there really shouldn't be any unexpected surprises, as there are recognizable and identifiable indicators to detect deterioration. Diminishing sales, tight cash flow and working capital show a clear picture of a troubled business.

Other factors contributing to a decline could be triggered off by dishonesty, change of key employees, supervision, inferior controls, competition, different suppliers' distribution policies, or a general weakened economy.

The earliest you discover any problems, the better the opportunity is to face the situation and react.

There were many times during my 38 years in operating a retail chain of stores that I put a moratorium on expenditures and set limits on any and all outlay of funds, except the bare necessities and creditors.

Your mind must constantly be tuned in to new ideas and opportunities and in depressed periods, change your merchandising trends to lower, maintain, and even increase income to meet the needs of the "times". Self-discipline is a trait that must be practiced to tie in with long hours and perseverance. Together with hard work, you must develop and create new ideas and innovations.

The difference of success or failure is proper timing and self-motivation. When the economy is on a downward trend the innovative entrepreneur will rise above the others. Search for your opportunity -- and you will find it, coming out "smelling like a rose" and rebuilding "par excellence". Don't hesitate to do it the way you are comfortable and confident.

Making firm decisions and good judgment can dispell failure to keep a company's survival. Mistakes can be costly but not fatal, and you must be ready for the task of changing your course of action.

Frequent Reasons for Business Decline

- Finding the wrong business

- Operating with only self leadership

- Poor management

- Unfamiliar with your market

- Mark-ups inadequate to generate a profit

- Insufficient cash flow

- Not being cognizant of competition

- Diminishing of shopping area.

Tips for Success

- Know your business

- Be thorough in planning

- Strategize before exerting energy and time

- Make your efforts count

- Be original and resourceful

- Study your market

- Stay current and updated with products

- Develop a high rapport with bankers, creditors, customers and employees

Methods of Business Assurance

- Carefully evaluate your business venture

- Study the need of your market product or service

- Concentrate on specialization

- Maintain adequate capital

- Operate within affordable expenses and controls

- Be flexible for cutbacks and downsizing

- Prepare your business for growth

On the brighter side, there are businesses that take a quick and sudden turn upward because they made the right decision at the proper time and grabbed the opportunity when it meant the most. They have no doubt watched when to act and when to sit back and wait. They have availed to themselves appropriate opportunities. Possibly some companies showed fast progress because of a change in trends and fashions and were there to take full advantage. Many adjusted their techniques to an updated method of operations.

Strong Attributes for Success

- Good background

- Sound manager

- Financial planners

- Merchandising ability

- Thorough thinker

- Understanding yourself

- Self motivator

- Enthusiastic

- Perseverance

- Persuasion

- Achiever

Failure can be an important ingredient to success. Don't expect the impossible dream that every move in a business is a direct maneuver to prosperity. Employees must be made to feel that their best efforts are important -- and be encouraged and motivated to feel comfortable in trying. Instill in them the will and desire to show initiative and be conscientious -- but a small blunder will not terminate the company -- and could be very helpful toward achievement and improvement. Practice makes perfect.

Defeat is such a threatening phase of business life that there are never enough warning signals to keep the business person on "his toes", cognizant and mindful of possibilities of disaster and desperation.

Remain prepared at all times and be ready to make changes when necessary. Frequent reasons for loss of performance and declining business are inadequate projections, lack of know-how, inefficiency and incapability. Precautionary measures to eliminate a breakdown are:

- Scrutinize proposed locations

- Develop sound market

- Do not over-expand

- Look for constant guidance in all facets of your operation

- Maintain information on a regular basis

- Poor leadership

- Be on guard against diminishing cash flow

- Be aware of loans and financing as to one's extension

- Poor financing arrangements

- Excess cost of financing

- Overlooking hazards

- Limited understanding of signs of regress

- Be promotional minded

- Always be aware of competitors' merchandising techniques

- Constant uplifting of employees

- Watch for trends and utilize information to your advantage.

Use all the above signals to control your everyday operation and your destiny by constant careful evaluations and studying in all areas.

Watching the above factors will assure you of the basic attributes prevailing upon yourself the opportunity of success. It will give you firm direction to maintain and build your business with a sound and solid foundation.

It is heartening to know that based on studies and statistics constantly taken by surveying companies, success over failure reigns a heavier percentage -- even though the downfall ratio is getting closer.

Keeping your eyes and ears open and taking the advantage when presented can make a difference. Appropriate help at the right time will sometimes change diversity for a struggling enterprise or company. Luck plays a part, but you have to make your own breaks.

It would be encouraging and helpful if when you experience problems in your business, you can turn to professional assistance to aid in the step before a possible disaster. The facts are that although the field of bankruptcy attorneys are adequate, there are very few consultants who practice guidance in business mismanagement and crucial direction to salvage a declining business. There are sufficient books, courses and seminars on all phases of business; however, there are few on survival.

A systematic and committed approach to the various facets of an operational structure must include every phase of the organizational procedures. Correction and inprovement on a step-by-step basis could mean the difference between success or failure.

Success in a business venture refers to survival stability and progress; whereas failure could be the ultimate end in the enterprise.

Operating a small business takes guts, courage, foresight and above all the patience, fortitude and hard work to meet the challenge for existence.

Strategies that Worked in My Business

Too many times I witnessed ups and down in my sales and ultimately quite a difference on profits or losses. Costly errors in any area, whether it be marketing, purchasing, operations or sales, can be devastating and fatal if not noticed early on. I constantly was on the lookout for any negative signs and always reacted immediately. There is no room for mental lapses.

I was always on guard for visible or hidden flaws as there is no place for any oversights. I constantly reviewed and made a study of every phase of my operation and was always ready to make improvements and changes.

During the course of my thirty-eight years in business, I had made four transitions -- changes in image, merchandising, marketing and operation. Each was a well thought out plan to improve success and guard against failure.

My first chance came about after World War II, following thirty years of my father having operated a small used clothing store. As a veteran, I took the opportunity and advantage of the benefits of war surplus and slowly purchased discarded merchandise until 1951 when the variety was conducive to an interesting concept. Then the original store was known as a surplus store. To move on toward success, I opened a similar store about every year until 1968 when continuing in a flourishing course, I saw another opportunity to push ahead.

The second transition to keep up with new merchandising ideas was noting the trend of outdoor living and leisure --

mostly as an outgrowth of the war. Fishing, and especially camping and hunting, were getting stronger in the 1960s -- so in 1968 all my shops were changed to "outdoor stores," specializing in these interests. This gave me the edge to continue into a successful direction. All my moods and merchandise became different with new decor and highlights.

Twelve years later in 1980, I saw the needs of people becoming more health, physical fitness and sports conscious, so my third transition to keep up with the times was taking the emphasis from the leisure field to sporting goods stores, with the accent on the variety of most ahtletic and exercise equipment, action footwear and apparel.

The fourth transition was relocating most stores from the inner city with limited traffic and purcahsing power to the major shopping malls to building volume and profit.

The above series of changes in my business was necessary for the anticipation of success and minimizing failure.

Lessons Learned

- *Stay on track for proper decisions.*

- *Face the challenges with real determination and appropriate action.*

- *Maintain a constant search for the right opportunities and development.*

CHAPTER 3

Fear of Bankruptcy

Prelude

Everyone in business faces ups and downs. The fear of bankruptcy enters the minds of those in a declining business so that the pressures and intensity exasperates. Eliminating the self destruction and building confidence for a successful self-reorganization is a herculean task.

People in business have a great deal invested in their enterprises. It could be lifes' savings, years of energies, sacrifice of time, and diversion of other opportunities.

A problem company basically has gotten itself in jeopardy because of ineffective management; customer reaction to poor service, and unacceptable products and costs which are out of line compared to value of the merchandise; and ineffective operations.

The longer the business has strived, earned profits, showing steady growth and stability, the harder it is to encounter a possible downfall when the tide is turned the other way. Facing the reality of a deteriorating business is generally tough to take.

Your early clue as to problems in your business will be a poor cash flow. After operating your company with monies flowing in and out on a regular smooth basis, having gained a reputation as always having been prompt pay, and then suddenly experience the unforeseen slow condition, will alarm you to the point of great concern.

Changing your style from comfort and calmness to a feeling of getting uptight and worry is a very traumatic sensation that you must adjust to cope with.

As you delve and explore further into reasons for your difficulty, your mind will be affected and you will become more cautious to evaluate your situation. This is when you have to grab hold of yourself, playing down the negative picture and think and act in a positive direction.

Most people do not react quick enough when the first signs of problems occur. As the financial position worsens and the facts become known with creditors and customers negatively responding to the situation, suddenly the picture becomes clearer and real.

The first thought going through the entrepreneur's mind is, "this can't happen to me". He won't believe his business is in that serious jeopardy, and his awakened new situation is slow to sink in. He doesn't take any additional precautions in operating his business and rolls along in his usual manner.

Suddenly, he sees the difference. Banks begin asking for more detailed and more frequent financial and status reports. Creditors tighten up their lines and employees' moral start dwindling and showing signs of concern.

Then his personality, mannerism and activities change. Actuality hits him hard, and his mind realizes the horror confronting him. Fear for devastation and downfall of his wavering business stand uppermost in his mind. As he becomes more and more frightened, the fear of bankruptcy dominates his thoughts twenty-four hours a day and clouds his vision.

Building your adrenalin to a peak in this situation can be a healthy response to assume and can give the faltering business the impetus it needs to fight back -- thereby having a counter effect to the fear of bankruptcy.

There are other choices in times of distress. Evaluating a plan which fits the needs of your company and individualized circumstance will help you choose the appropriate direction for survival. Review all the possibilities with bankruptcy as the last recourse.

Eliminating the self destruction of the fear of bankruptcy and pointing your emphasis toward self-reorganization will take a lot of thought and effort, but the results could be very rewarding. It may not be the easy way out, but a well planned and conscientious program can be very successful.

The best alternative in reorganizing your business is to do it yourself. It requires a great effort, a tremendous challenge and the best opportunity for future stability. This step before bankruptcy will establish restored credibility and a renewed rapport and respect from your business world.

The art of self-reorganization mandates a strong commitment to personally involve yourself in every facet of your business -- to thoughtfully evaluate, "tear down" and rebuild each and every part of the operation.

Bankers, creditors, customers, service people and employees all must be dealt with on an individual and analytical basis.

Repayment of debts, eliminating excessive interest charges and looking to profits is a herculean task, but the opportunity to succeed in this endeavor makes it all worthwhile.

Strategies that Worked in My Business

I am the first to admit and acknowledge the fears through the years of taking continual risks to "hold your own" and try to forge ahead. There is no such thing as "status quo" in business as one must constantly make changes requiring on-going modifications and expenses. Generally this necessitates additional monies and investments which puts many businesses in a precarious position for downfall or bankruptcy, unless a surplus of funds has been accumulated.

My continuous need for additional funds and supplies from creditors and bankers to keep up expansion goals, kept my adrenalin flowing, more intense input of energy and time; and a deeper concern of sustenance and survival.

At all times, these pressures enhanced my abilities to shop better; to build a keener and more effective operation; to merchandise in a more modern and sophisticated manner; to use more ingenuity to shop for merchandise; and to convince my bankers for their financial support.

Leon Albin

I feel that with my courage and self-made fear of destruction, I sustained myself and my business.

Lessons Learned

- *Be honest with yourself -- face the "worst case" scenario and plan from there.*

- *Monitor your cash flow as a "barometer" of your business health.*

- *Try to keep an instant calmness in dealing with the outside.*

- *Focus on the positive -- play down the negative.*

- *Do not let fear cloud your judgment.*

- *Let the adrenalin flow become a positive force for change.*

- *Be well thought out and plan carefully.*

- *Take control of your reins.*

CHAPTER 4

Stay Strong and Composed

Prelude

Keep yourself in a good mental state by maintaining a level head and a positive outlook. This will give you the strength to put forth your best ability to get over the hurdles necessary to make a comeback.

There are many aspects and various facets to work toward survival of a business. The entire operation is intertwined with one another to keep it together.

Whether it is purchasing, merchandising, distribution, selling, employee relationship and morale, financing or management, the big key is being able to do all the above necessary functions with the most expertise possible. Everyone's best performance can only be obtained if your mind and body are clear of stress and pain.

Whether you are faced with business or personal problems, you must not bring them in the work place. You must condition yourself to stay strong and composed and focus on your strengths. It is contagious and people working around you will look to you as an example for leadership. One bad apple creates many more -- and you must be the one to follow so that the organization works at its best, and gets the most out of every area possible.

A "strong" reason you enjoy being a small business person is the feeling of independence doing your own thing. To extend this pride to your employees will give them the enthusiasm and motivation to help your company. This feeling of belonging and being part of can stand out as much as any other remuneration of salary or any other fringe benefits.

Your interest and desire for change and improvement requires movement by company management.

Learning and benefitting by mistakes and applying vision with experience will strengthen the future and survival of your business.

Always be prepared to adjust to improve any failures, errors or oversights and encourage within your organization the ability and desire to correct and improve, constantly search for set-backs, and instill the spirit of teamwork to remedy any situation.

All organizations run into faulty procedures and methods - - but it is those companies that recognize and learn from their errors that move forwards to a higher level.

Obviously the more expeditiously we change direction, the better our gains and progress will be. It is therefore incumbent on management to arouse by stimulating the feeling and desire in working together. Discourage and displace apprehension and uneasiness with courage and foresight. Develop continuous incentives and goals along the way.

Management must lead by example and generate and produce ideas and programs acceptable and workable by the entire organization. Define each phase to be understandable to perform.

Effects of the causes are directly dependent on the correctable habits and procedures following its evaluation and study. Building profit in your business is based on your ability to utilize and improve upon the factors of better cost, controls and operation.

Contributing circumstances of the economy, market and governmental authorities directly influence your business and must be watched closely. Follow up all opportunities in a timely fashion and take advantage of circumstances for gains and progress. Pay close attention to the market and always be aware of customer needs and relations. Leadership and motivation must stay in the forefront.

Keeping yourself above water requires strong will-power and determination and having a level head will give you a clear mind to think, act at your best, and not to abandon the ship. It takes guts, perserverance and staying power. It rubs off to others, so lead the way. Be patient, sit back and let nature take its toll and think before you react. You will need a change of attitude and leadership and a hard nose approach to survive.

Empower your foresight with strong drive and a positive outlook as to your ability to handle the problems. Make every act and decision work in the right direction, displaying sturdy ambition to succeed. Remember, if you don't try, you won't make any mistakes -- but you will not make any progress, and vision will be curtailed.

Strategies that Worked in My Business

Somehow or other I was able to work better under pressure. So many times during my thirty-eight years in business I had to grit my teeth and "hold back" the steam. In the midst of numerous transactions and negotiations, people would lose control, but more often than not I found I was able to make my point by keeping cool and showing restraint. Even though some people fly off the handle, they respected those that kept a level head. Not responding back to their rage generally gave me the edge to feel confident and have the advantage in making a deal.

When the thought first came to my mind of making a change in my business from the old surplus image to an updated leisure field merchandising of camping, fishing and hunting, many suppliers were very pessimistic to my transition. Their feelings were that it was very risky and many discouraged me for lack of experience and financial backing to outfit this new look and extensive merchandise needs.

Of course, most of the vendors were helpful and gave me the encouragement to handle the others. There were enough manufacturers and distributors, however, that tried to push me to the limit by not cooperating with the credit necessary for my new lines to round out my outdoor stores. Some sales representatives didn't visit or make calls to me as they felt I was under-capitalized to make my moves. The discouragement was evident and disheartening.

Staying strong and composed, never displaying any tempers, showing confidence in my ability and goals slowly convinced every supplier to sell me the lines and even worked hard and long with me for sales aids, displays, and merchandising.

Lessons Learned

- *Don't let your problems dilute your ability to perform.*
- *Demonstrate your strong leadership to encourage others in your battle for survival.*
- *Keep a level head and set an example for others to follow.*

CHAPTER 5

Work Out a Plan

Prelude

The most important phase of a business turnaround is to work out a plan back to a successful road. Planning a good and sound direction is the first step. Every facet of your business must be included to effect this project to working out the problems and to come up with solutions.

Counteracting fear, one must have self-assurance. Building resistance and keeping level-headed will bring on the stamina to put all your faculties together to work up a plan for survival. When you are faced with the dilemma of a backward trend, get on the defensive and reach furiously for something to hold. You must immediately execute and administer a method to proceed and steady your company in an appropriate path to get things back to normal and forthright. Small business has its many ups and downs -- and those who understand and work out the setbacks become the survivors. Every crisis and each predicament should have a scheme to overcome an adverse situation. Likewise, ideas for progress must be well thought out. In fact, no move should begin without first developing the entire procedure.

In order to put together an effective work plan in a declining business, you must examine the problem and act in an aggressive manner to overcome these obstacles. Do not rush this process, and prepare updated information of sales figures, expenses and evaluation of personnel in order to make appropriate and timely decisions. Be extremely thorough in making your deliberations, followed by action. Organize your people to participate in this project; delegate their responsibilities; and impress on them the importance of a profitable business and their integral part to make it a success.

In re-evaluating your overall business, the entire structure must be re-examined, putting strong emphasis on cutbacks, unprofitable areas and obsolete and costly departments.

You cannot afford to have a long term process. You must set up stages and strive to make each step successful. As you struggle and work out each part of the proposal, progress will ultimately prevail.

Do not hesitate to recreate your organization by changing job duties and responsibilities and even elimination of positions and non-productive employees. Rebuilding could require bringing in outsiders to turn the company around.

Clear and explicit direction must be given to the personnel responsible to meet the survival needs and it is imperative to determine a practice of scrutinizing all reports and results of each department.

It is to no one's best interest to close your doors. Tax authorities, bankers and creditors will always react favorably to any indebtedness -- if you demonstrate sincere efforts of good intentions. Usually all interested and affected parties will arrange to talk and meet with you to help salvage your situation. You must, however, be very careful that no one dominates too great of your limited revenues, but a spread must be taken into consideration to satisfy everyone due money. It is a natural undertaking to want to accommodate those who have a tighter hold on your destiny -- either by collateral or laws of protection. However, they too realize that working up any unsatisfactory and unrealistic ideas will jeopardize their possibilities for collection of their maximums. It is to their advantage to help you keep "the wolves" away.

A good work out plan should be realistic, based on projected budgeting of income and expenses; and commitments must be made with deep study, evaluation, and good faith.

Strategy does not always mean repayment of 100% of the debt -- even over long periods of time. This, of course, is the ultimum -- but if conditions of the business do not dictate this -- negotiations for discounts or portions will be entertained.

Do not hestitate to offer a one lump discounted payment, a monthly figure to each party based on the above -- whether it is a 100% payback over a period of years or a reasonable long discounted commitment.

In some cases, suppliers will forgive a debt if special arrangements and commitment are made for future business on a C.O.D. basis. Other times a reimbursement could be extended if remitted over a period while continuing buisness on a pay-as-you-go plan.

In addition to extending terms for payables, some firms will consider converting the debt to a note or might even consider your purchases on a consignment basis -- eliminating their risk by maintaining ownership.

Professional guidance would probably be needed to accomplish this important phase of budgeting and payback of a work out undertaking.

You must have cash to stay in business. Therefore, your cash flow statements will be your key to existence. Further, all other data is pertinent for your direction. Close scrutiny and evaluation of accounting, personnel, sales and purchasing become more important than ever before in your making day to day decisions. Everything counts toward your revival. Be sure that all information is accurate so as to be in a position to make the proper decisions. Be fair but firm in your resolutions.

On a regular basis, review your project to be sure it is on target and working the way it was intended. This valuable step to strengthen your position must be constantly watched and modified as necessary to maintain your direction. Your performance must be discussed frequently with professionals so as to meet your goals.

All phases of your operation must be part of your design to cover every facet of your day-to-day activities. Proper information will guide you on necessary changes in marketing, purchasing, distribution, sales, administrative, employees, customers and any other area.

In considering all of the above, follow closely each part, and make every attempt to improve day-to-day and alter your tactics when necessary.

There are certain red flags that must be addressed and rectified to counteract a setback: turnover of merchandise, controlled debts and expenses, receivables due, and bank credit. These are the key issues to be dealt with to successfully adopt a procedure, and each category must be cost-effective.

Devastating problems in a busniess are caused if financial statements are not kept current; excessive dead inventory is on hand, there are excessive perks; and cash flow is less than expense.

Most businesses realize they must work out a recovery scheme if conditions reach a critical stage. Too small of a portion of businesses prepare their thoughts to handle unexpected situations and are in no position to react if trouble occurs. Pre-planning should be part of the business approach

-- and if done properly can be their key to managing an emergency.

Salvaging a troubled business on self-preservation or liquidation on your own will benefit both debtor and creditor. The step before bankruptcy can be a very exasperating, yet rewarding experience. Make a firm decision to put very rigid and disciplined thoughts together with your own personnel and also outside assistance; then a determined and aggressive commitment to follow through with a working team will give you the opportunity of eliminating bankruptcy and accomplish a re-organization that can produce the acceptable end result.

Convincing your creditors, suppliers and banker is a selling chore, but if you have always shown dignity, responsibility and credibility, your chances to convince them to be patient, tolerant and cooperative are good.

Chronic problems do not go away unless faced with solutions to resolve the circumstances, whether it's the financial lender, the creditors, the organization or employees. Situations must be handled without delay to reduce further downfall.

Recognizing the shortcomings in your enterprise can be done with an affordable and skilled consultant who specializes in the field of turnarounds. This assistance can be used sparingly and on a limited basis -- but could be the difference for the right direction.

Evaluate if your business is in a distressful situation by studying the following situations to determine if you need to seek assistance:

- Steady decrease in sales
- Expenses increasing
- Too many markdowns on your inventory
- Obsolete financial information
- Under-capitalization

- Falling behind on bank loan repayments and creditor payables

- Over-extension of supplier credit

- Diverting payroll and withholding expenses

- Applying constant "band-aids".

To help lessen the above problems, action must be taken to attempt to correct. The most practical method would be to seek outside professional assistance. They would be in a better neutral and acceptable position to deal with your bankers, creditors and suppliers. They will further assist in debt consolidation and credit extension. Their expertise, together with your knowledge of your business, would help extensively to alleviate your deplorable situation.

In order to begin the exerted efforts for a business turnaround, you must have a full picture and evaluation as to what your true status is. Define your posture clearly and face your facts and position to make a change and an upward swing to accomplish a realistic goal.

Create an agenda which will allow you to complete your program in fairly quick order. Study all aspects of needed changes, taking into account suppliers, employees and customers.

Prepare yourself for the stress and strain for the efforts you will be faced with. This tension will be lightened if you arrange to obtain adequate data and facts to give you a basis to analyze every aspect you are attempting to improve. Put together a good team, and especially involve your employees in the project. Work toward building a stronger organization which will strengthen your purpose toward profits and progress.

The main purpose of a business turnaround is to review the reasons for the company's decline. Then, steps must be taken to improve the leadership in order to change and improve current procedures.

Strong decisions and new ideas must be made very quickly, which will help the profit structure by increasing volume and decreasing expenses. All employees must be involved to perfect your endeavors. Give them the opportunity to share and being part of your new goals.

Full and thorough thoughts in working up a plan must be made before you begin.

- Have an extensive understanding as to the current problems.
- Put together what has to be done to remedy.
- Set your aims to be doable.
- Produce steps to reach goals within projected time constraints.
- Estimate dates of completion.
- Monitor the plan as it progresses.
- Change and alter if necessary.

Designing ideas must include certain basic essentials for involvement:

- Consider the input and expertise of the players (personnel).
- Be certain that those counted on as integral parts of the plan are being paid to put forth full dedication.
- Know your market.
- Shoppers must feel comfortable and satisfied.
- Feel satisfied and comfortable with your financial institutions.

Developing your own plan for reorganization requires strong fortitude and conviction. Study the following needs to give you direction:

1. Evaluate your entire operation and make changes where necessary. Responsibilities in all areas must be

studied for weaknesses and no hesitation should hold up necessary substitutions.

2. Scrutinize and correct controls to uncover weaknesses in record keeping.

3. Pay closer attention to monthly comparative financial statements.

4. Soften your credit problems by more realistic calculations of a cash projection so as to repay creditors on a more timely basis. Keep them informed as to expected payment plan.

5. Re-evaluate your pricing structure, so as to be competitive, yet still have adequate margins.

6. Re-visit your advertising agenda to be sure you are not wasting dollars and that these expenditures are covering your intended market.

7. Sell off dead stock, maintain more updated merchandise for a faster inventory turnover.

8. Tighten up purchasing procedures.

9. Scrutinize very closely all operational expenses and eliminate or reduce when feasible.

10. Depend more on reliable employees to improve.

11. Establish a close rapport with key people in your organization to study progress and watch for warning signals.

12. Build up closer ties with professionals.

In addition to a total dedication by the head of the company, all interested and affected parties involved in a turnaround project must be convinced that the head of the company is totally committed to make the plan work. Also, that the negotiation team has ability, enthusiasm, determination, conscientiousness and sincerity.

Strategies that Worked in My Business

I can relate countless times that working out a plan kept my business surviving. There were two that stand out which required complete and thorough creativity. Both were in the area of consolidation.

The first was when I changed from surplus stores to outdoor stores. I had to move and replace older locations to other areas or change the present stores to the new look and concept conducive to the leisure type merchandise. It was necessary to stretch out a theme; travel to new markets; have sales representatives set up training classes to learn the new products; and adapt to the new trade and customers.

It was no easy task because it required a radical change and format to accomplish my goal while maintaining my sales volume without a heavy increased expense factor.

Related to the above thought and consolidated experience was at the time I decided to sell my chain of stores. I had already made another transition from the outdoor stores to full line sporting goods stores. The buyers who I had tentatively made a deal with only wanted selected mall locations and stores which fit into their operation with no inventory. It was therefore incumbent on me to sell off the inventory, buy off some leases to close stores, merge others, and rent additional stores. Further, I had to satisfy all creditors, landlords, and loans. All this was necessary to consolidate the chain to the core they wanted.

I knew this was to be complicated, but with the appropriate procedures, I felt very confident and had no doubt as to the final outcome.

Since my banker was the biggest "backer" in my business, I met with him to discuss my planned activity. After being assured and giving his bank further protection of their interest, he cooperated and allowed me to sell off the inventory. Next, of course, my creditors had to be made aware so they could be comfortable. Then, I organized sales at sacrificed prices and closings where applicable to meet my cash needs for creditors and reduction of stores to fulfill the agreement.

Based on a solid plot to be executed, and followed by an organized and cooperated effort by all involved, my goals were achieved.

Consolidation does not only apply to closing and merging stores, but also is utilized in unloading and selling off obsolete merchandise, raising cash, or improving your operation.

Lessons Learned

You should develop a plan that includes:

- *Forecast cash payments to creditors that can be supported by business cash flow.*

- *Share information with creditors.*

- *Special arrangements with creditors.*

- *Evaluate plans for personnel and sales force.*

- *Conduct interim reviews.*

- *Present payment alternatives.*

- *Develop an on-going strategy.*

CHAPTER 6

Forecasting and Budgeting

Prelude

> *You must be tuned into what your goals are for the future. Gathering proper information is the key to sound and usable forecasting for proper direction in managing and controlling your business.*

Projecting for the future -- whether it be one month, one year or five years down the road -- is an essential leg to a successful business. Planning ahead is a good habit in all matters of life, but organizing systematic steps in your business eliminates surprises and gives you an edge toward your goals.

As you continue month-to-month to make these calculations, your knowledge and estimates will get sharper and sharper. This is the guidance you will get to depend on which will become helpful as the monthly forecast is done.

Forecasting will show your slow periods when extra funds are needed for cash flow so as to prepare for necessary loans or other methods of generating cash.

Knowing when these slow times historically affect your business will put you on guard to controlling disbursements. It will keep you informed as to attempts to defer payments until later or when seasons occur with higher sales.

Demonstrating foresight will avail to you, your creditors, banker and key assitants the information to target your aims and goals. They are forerunners as necessary ingredients to your decisions and accomplishments. The budgeting information will alert you as to the flexibility and rigidness to follow in your plan of action. Sensible anticipation will allow you the feasibility to level and strike a balance to meet your estimations.

Preparing for the future is essential to project where your business is going, gives you a good picture of what you should expect, and how to react if the trend doesn't look encouraging. Also, it will give you proper ideas of when and how to expand based on information available to you. Once you formulate your habit to consider this part of your management process, you will not operate without it.

Forecasting as an Integral Tool for Management

Planning for day to day functions will help manage the activities in your business. Consider the following for future aid:

- Build confidence in your projections.
- Open up thoughts and ideas as to needs in your business.
- Predict working capital needed to operate.
- Keep yourself aware of your profit and loss status.
- Maintain timely information as to expected income and expenses.
- Put out "red flags" as warnings.

- Be aware of your cash predicament.

- Obtain a better picture as to where and how to use your money.

- Be knowledgeable of cost.

- Allow bankers and creditors to feel more comfortable.

A true study of your cash position allows you to make proper decisions in all aspects of your business. It takes into consideration cash on hand less monies needed.

Understanding the steps of the basics will allow you to be in a position of knowing your cash status. It will keep you aware of your present situation as well as daily funds required. It will alert you as to when to look for additional financial support. Regular cash analysis will help make the difference for your company's sound decision making.

Very little happens unless you concentrate and exert your efforts to make it come to pass. Forecasting not only gives you the opportunity to face head-on ensuing problems and to adjust to change, but also gives you the ability to build forward for growth.

Projections can be simplified into limited key categories for concentration. A workable plan will give you a profile of your business; can be designed internally to fit your own needs; and should be a guide to be referred to and followed.

The first area to examine is where are we going with sales -- and how can we build this volume. Whether it be with current inventory, new products, cutting prices, increasing prices, updated displays, a new look in your business, or better customer service. Each part ties into a sales boost and deserves individual attention. They all play an important part, and the more energy and time you put into it will be directly relevant to the growth you are anticipating.

A market survey will clarify the opportunities. It will indicate where your products are most acceptable and will point out to you pricing against competition. It will also reveal to you the people you are trying to reach and if your lines are adaptable to their needs and wants.

As important to building sales is the ability to put a hold on expenses. Therefore the budgeting aspect must be studied and carefully scrutinized to control the entire picture in order to expand the bottom line -- profit.

Cost control is directly related to your planning of sales. The ultimate utopia would be if receipts can be increased while outlays could be decreased. Dealing with budgeting of expenses does not necessarily mean that they must be reduced. If additional monies are needed for more sales, consider accordingly and don't go overboard. Be careful not to build your staff out of proportion so as to eat up the contemplated expansion before you even start.

Plan to limit your spending budget. Be very cognizant of waste and duplication. Reduce where possible to build the bottom line.

Leon Albin

Strategies that Worked in My Business

Predicting the future in my business was a rather easy task because we kept an excellent history of past performance. Throughout the many years, forecasting and budgeting played an important role in my decision making.

For six months, I had been negotiating for my seventh store. Discussions were at an impasse and another place presented itself, which I decided to commit to. One week later, the owner of the other site called and accepted my offer. This put me in a precarious position, because I was really eager for that location. I asked for, and received, a week to give him an answer if I would accept.

Of course, all my reviews and studies had already been done evaluating the practicality of the site and its potential. Everything was reviewed regarding adaptability with our present chain, management, expectations and affordability. It met the full test and I was completely satisfied to move forward.

Along came this other opportunity and a location I thought would be a natural. Previous to this, I have never opened more than one store a year, and this would require all the planning and preparations at the same time. Of course, the benefit of opening both on the same day would save on advertising expenses.

The prudent thing to do at this point was to go back to the "drawing board," use all the information gathered for the first store and duplicate all facts for a possible second store; then putting the two together to appraise the risk of the two undertakings at once.

The first part of the new review was whether or not our workforce could handle the load of preparing for two store openings. This would include design, fixturing, merchandise distribution and displays. Transferring approximately fifteen percent of inventory from each current store together with the anticipated purchases would fill and supply the appropriate product mix needed.

Double expenses raised some concerns, but we were able to counteract this by squeezing the variable expenses throughout the chain. Of course, fixed expenses remained as they were. The re-assignment of one personnel from each current store would give us the depth of experience with the new employees hired. Last, but by no means least of the analysis, was anticipated sales to withstand the entire venture of the two store openings.

I was very contented with my findings and concluded with encouragement and optimism that it was the appropriate move. I then called the owner of the first property and signed the lease. Both stores were opened at the same time and in less than six months were an integral part of our company.

Lessons Learned

- *Systematic planning is a key to business success.*

- *Forecasting is a methodology that will provide a road map for the future by highlighting what to expect and how to react to changes.*

- *The forecast should take into account for both sides of the income statement -- revenues and expenses.*

- *Revenue forecast should consider capacity, seasonability, pricing, strategy, customers.*

- *Expense forecast should include costs, overhead, labor, rent, etc.*

Three-Month Cash Receipts Projection Worksheet

Sample for Each Quarter

	MONTH 1		MONTH 2		MONTH 3	
	PROJECTION	ACTUAL	PROJECTION	ACTUAL	PROJECTION	ACTUAL
BEGINNING CASH BALANCE						
Plus: Receipts						
Cash Sales						
Credit Sales Collection:						
0-30 Days						
31-60 Days						
61-90 Days						
Over 90 Days						
Other Income						
Cash Receipts Sub-Total						
TOTAL CASH AVAILABLE						
DISBURSEMENTS						
Cash Purchases						
Credit Purchases						
0-30 Days						
31-60 Days						
Over 60 Days						

(continued)

	MONTH 1		MONTH 2		MONTH 3	
	PROJECTION	ACTUAL	PROJECTION	ACTUAL	PROJECTION	ACTUAL
Total General, Administrative and Selling Expenses						
Equipment Purchases:						
Loan Principal Payments						
Other						
TOTAL CASH DISBURSEMENTS						
CASH SURPLUS (DEFICIT)						
Min. Cash Balance Required						
Bank Loan Required Short-Term						
CASH ENDING BALANCE						

GENERAL ADMINISTRATIVE AND SELLING EXPENSES SCHEDULE

Sample for Each Quarter

	MONTH 1		MONTH 2		MONTH 3	
	BUDGET	ACTUAL	BUDGET	ACTUAL	BUDGET	ACTUAL
OPERATING EXPENSES						
Salaries (Owners)						
Salaries (Employees)						
Taxes (Payroll)						
Rent						
Advertising						
Telephone						
Insurance						
Professional Fees						
Repairs & Maintenance						
Office Expense						
Utilities						
Taxes (Other)						

(continued)

	MONTH 1		MONTH 2		MONTH 3	
	BUDGET	ACTUAL	BUDGET	ACTUAL	BUDGET	ACTUAL
Travel & Entertainment						
Dues & Subscriptions						
TOTAL GENERAL AND ADMINISTRATIVE EXPENSES						
Depreciation						
TOTAL OPERATING EXPENSES						

CHAPTER 7

Improving Cash Flow

Prelude

Your sustenance and survival is dependent on the working capital and surplus created by cash flow. Sound cash management is the key to operational success and you must train and discipline yourself with basic principles to create funds.

The lifeblood of your sustenance is working capital or commonly known as cash flow. Businesses cannot afford or tolerate the loss of cash, inventory or receivables.

Cash flow management is the most significant factor to succeed in business. Being the most important component of working capital makes it mandatory for your daily successful performance. These are the first numbers that suppliers and bankers observe on your statements for consideration of credit and financing.

The ability to retain a flourishing business is directly related to your maintaining money on hand. Having adequate funds to employ capable personnel, stock your shelves and advertise your products requires working capital. This is the net difference of income less disbursements.

Cash flow creates the needed working, capital surplus funds and the equity needed for survival and progress.

Cash is the energy which keeps the business in operation. It dictates your strengths and weaknesses. Good accounting and management systems can make the difference between a profit or loss in your business.

Even though your statements might show a paper profit; nevertheless, the "hard" cash is what the business thrives on. Paper profit is not the strength behind your success. You must have the ability to operate and curtail your profits and build capital. You cannot count your receivables as readily usable funds to spend on a current basis. Distinguish the current funds available as opposed to monies on the books.

Cash flow can be improved and maintained by controlling excessive and unneeded equipment and inventory. Obsolescence must be eliminated or cut back to increase your funds.

Records must be kept current in order for your financial condition to be available on a regular basis of either weekly or monthly. A recap can be done as simple or as detailed as warranted to accomplish the information desired, including making you aware of your breakeven or profitability point. It should contain sales, purchases, expenses, net profit and working capital.

Money problems are not only created by lack of sales or over-expenditures, but can be exasperated by over-expansion and untimely growth. You should not undermine your necessary working capital for your progress, but rather you should look to surplus funds, available loans and outside investors.

At your first signs of a crisis, where your creditors are affected and you find taxes, payroll and shipments in jeopardy, you must immediately take action to face this crunch. You must generate money at any expense to create funds for your limited on-going needs. Use your ingenuity to promote a sale with identifiable reduced prices; be extremely stingy and economical on all expenses or pay-outs, and begin your movement on stretching your dollars, including creditor payments.

After determining the amount of reserves needed to "stop the bleeding" and heal the wound, the methods described in this chapter may fall short of raising the appropriate dollars. It may be necessary to go one step further to tap internal sources of relatives and friends.

In conjunction with the above, a sound management team and operation is of profound importance to produce the liquidity necessary for building funds.

Most business failures are a result of inadequate cash flow. Troubled businesses always run into this problem, which is the beginning of many difficult days to follow. Squeezing out workable funds to operate and continue makes it imperative to be extremely frugal, shaving as much as possible.

More frequent turnover will build surplus flawlessly and painlessly since there is no increased inventory needed. In fact, concentration on unloading slower or dead stock with promotions or sales will add to the upsurge of working capital and create availability for faster turning merchandise.

The portion of your sales which are sold with credit could dissipate your dollars if they are not reimbursed promptly. If your purchases are due and payable before your accounts receivable are collected, it is hindering your liquid position. You cannot afford to carry accounts receivables on an extended basis. Your sales could be high, but if the receipt of your monies are slow, it could be harmful. Building a heavy inventory to support aged receivables is bad business. In direct relation, it will place your business in a slow position of payment to your creditors.

Produce more stringent restrictions on extending credit. You must exert efforts to get paid on a faster pace. Consider shorter terms, create discounts, incentives, and accept credit cards. Also give thought to deposits with orders.

To evaluate your cash flow, start by analyzing and studying your problematical areas. Review the list as often as monthly, but never longer than quarterly. Look closely at the variable expenses which can be controlled and lessened and concentrate on improving this element of your management program. Be objective, realistic and forceful. Make it happen.

A detailed knowledge and study of the accounting of available funds is necessary to perfect a sound cash management undertaking. You must have a grasp of this necessary operating component to avail yourself the opportunity of replenishing monies when needed.

Determining your requirements is directly related to your knowledge of cash on hand, sales projection and any other income expected. Further, you must take into consideration any money which will become attainable by selling off of any fixed assets or equities.

A hard-nose approach to your receivables will generate cash. Also review very objectively the liquidation or selling off and tightening some assets for cash.

Selling off certain stores for the inventory to create working capital when in a pinch is a unique approach to fill a void when you have reached your credit limit with the bank, or you hesitate to approach them because of unimpressive statements. You must use further ingenuity to generate funds.

In my business, heavy capital (at least for my status) was needed. There were periods when sales were slow, inventory was needed, and expenses, of course, were constant. I had to come up with some "ingenuity" to keep things going.

Rather than jeopardizing my entire chain of stores -- here is how I put new blood: through the years, I would earmark a store based on poor history as "no future" and put together a program to close that store. I would create additional cash by a "Lost Our Lease Sale" and then the remaining inventory would be moved and fit into other stores to fill their needs. It's an art not only to open stores but also to close them.

Concentrating on pushing sales while creating better inventory management and controls will further enhance your position.

To further strengthen your balance sheet or cash on hand, approach certain creditors to consider conversion to notes payable or conversion to consignment. Also, thought can be given to converting ownership to leasing.

Another method of raising money is liquidating assets which are not needed or are dispensable to the continuance of the operation.

If there are past due accounts on the books, a special attempt can be to reduce these receivables and raising funds by offering special discounts for prompt payments.

Management of cash flow and setting strict guidelines will avail the proper amount needed to meet your obligations; both for creditors as well as all necessary expenses to operate your business.

After you have "skinned the cat" and gotten rid of all the pork in your operation, study other areas to build cash flow to survive. Study your equipment and other assets where you might be able to cut back and unload to build up your balances. Unused real property is always something to consider to dispose.

Being in a pinch for cash, resort to every method and resource possible, but by all means tie in this project with sound management policies.

PROCEDURES FOR CASH MANAGEMENT

- Familiarize your cash flow cycle to understand working capital needs.

- Maintain monthly forecasting budget.

- Study your profit and loss statements on a regular basis.

- Deposit monies on a daily basis.

- Maintain adequate bank balances.

- Any accounts receivables must be invoiced promptly.

- Do not carry lengthy overdue accounts. Seek collection assistance as soon as possible.

- Maintain an inventory which turns over.

- Discount purchases as much as possible.

- Lease equipment if available, instead of outright purchases.

- Classify employees on a regular basis so as not to carry "dead wood".

Monthly Cash Flow Analysis and Projection

CASH RECEIPTS (Accounts Receivable)	$	
CASH RECEIPTS (Cash Sales)		
TOTAL CASH AVAILABLE	$	
MONTHLY EXPENSES:		
Purchases for Resale	$	
Rent		
Salaries (Owner)		
Salaries (Employees)		
Payroll Taxes		
Professional Fees		
Advertising		
Office Expenses		
Insurance		
Utilities		

(continued)

Supplies		
Telephone		
Auto Expenses		
Miscellaneous		
Loan Payments (Principal)		
Loan Payments (Interest)		
Other Loans		
TOTAL MONTHLY EXPENSE	$	
CASH FLOW FOR MONTH	$	

Three Month Projection

Cash Flow Projection	FIRST MONTH	SECOND MONTH	THIRD MONTH
Period:			
BEGINNING CASH	$	$	$
CASH RECEIPTS			
TOTAL CASH AVAILABLE	$	$	$
EXPENSES:			
Payments on Old Payables	$	$	$
Purchases: Current Month			
Rent			
Salaries (Employees)			
Salaries (Owner)			
Payroll Taxes			
Professional Fees			
Advertising			
Office Expense			

(continued)

Insurance					
Utilities					
Supplies					
Telephone					
Auto Expense					
Miscellaneous					
Loan Payments (Principal)					
Loan Payments (Interest)					
Other Loans					
TOTAL CASH PAID OUT	$	$	$		
ENDING CASH	$	$	$		

Three Month Projection

Cash Flow Variance Report

For Month of:

Cash Flow Variance Report	Projection	Actual	Variance
BEGINNING CASH	$	$	$
CASH RECEIPTS			
TOTAL CASH AVAILABLE	$	$	$
EXPENSES:			
Payments to Vendors on Old Payables	$	$	$
Purchases: Current Month			
Rent			
Salaries (Employees)			
Salaries (Owner)			
Payroll Taxes			
Professional Fees			
Advertising			
Office Expenses			
Insurance			

(continued)

Utilities			
Supplies			
Telephone			
Auto Expense			
Miscellaneous			
Loan Payments (Principal)			
Loan Payments (Interest)			
Other Loans			
TOTAL CASH PAID OUT	$	$	$
ENDING CASH	$	$	$

Projected Monthly Expenses
(Twelve Month Period)

	Jan	Feb	Mar	Apr	May	Jun	Jul	Aug	Sep	Oct	Nov	Dec	TOTALS
INCOME													
Sales													
Other													
TOTAL INCOME													
EXPENSES													
Salaries													
Purchases													
Rent													
Advertising													
Utilities													
Travel and Entertainment													
Dues & subscriptions													
Insurance													
Licenses													
Legal and accounting													
Office expenses													
Freight													
Postage													

(continued)

Repairs, maintenance											
Supplies											
Sales tax											
Taxes											
Telephone											
Interest expense											
Auto expense											
TOTAL EXPENSES											
NET INCOME (Income - Expenses)											

Strategies that Worked in My Business

I have had instances, like most businesses, when sales lagged, economic conditions were affected, and with expenses continuing, raising cash became critical in order to meet obligations.

One year before I actually merged and sold my chain of stores, I realized a very serious cash flow problem. I knew I had to do something very drastic and unique to turn my inventory into funds. I needed money fast. I had to lower my debts.

I had to come up with an idea for a sale which would have a great impact, attract people to our stores, build big revenues, yet not hurt our image. I could not afford to bring in new merchdndise or sell off at a sacrifice any inventory which would have to be replaced.

The fastest and most desirable line of items we stocked was athletic footwear. It also comprised the largest variety and heaviest dollar investment. I had the stores inventory our shoes in categories, made a thorough study of the length of time that each type were on the shelves, studied the turnover in classifications, and evaluated footwear dollars invested as to sales of the previous six months compared to all the other lines. It clearly showed an abundance of stock, and even though it was our fastest class of merchandise, it also revealed that the ratios were way out in contrast to the others.

After this careful review, it became very obvious and apparent as to what had to be done -- a gigantic and huge clearance of our athletic shoe department, including "all" men's, women's and children's. Every shoe visible in the stores would be sacrificed at ridiculous and unheard of prices.

Shoes which were purchased within the last two months were considered current models and taken off sale and stocked in the back rooms. The other excess and obsolete shoes were displayed on visible tables throughout the center. A large sign covered each store's front "clearance of all shoes 40% - 70% off." Similar signs were on each table as well as sale pennants throughout the stores. Also, newspaper and radio ads ran with the same theme.

The sale ran for thirty days and was unbelievable. Not only did it clear out massive aged inventory, but it produced more than the cash flow expected. Over 10,000 pairs of shoes were sold amounting to over $150,000. This was by far the most successful sale I ever had in my thirty-eight years of business.

Lessons Learned

- *You must take a strategic approach to raising cash.*
- *Look at all potential sources to generating cash, including:*
- *Selling slow moving inventory.*
- *Selling non-productive assets.*
- *Quicken receivables collection cycle.*
- *Slow down the payables cycle.*
- *Increase inventory turns.*
- *Increase cash sales and reduce credit sales.*

CHAPTER 8

The Pay-Out Schedule

Prelude

When cash becomes a major problem, spread out your funds to creditors to make an attempt to pacify as many as possible. Work up a system for periodic pay-outs commensurate with your flow of money. Be realistic with your projections.

When business is going down and cash flow becomes almost non-existent, together with heavy bills, it becomes very frightening. You become very distressful and wonder how you will be able to pay bills that have occurred, and if there will be any funds available to keep things going.

Having had the fine reputation and the pleasure of always having been prompt in paying your bills, the sudden difficulty of meeting your obligations could be a shock you must absorb. Before you consider the pay-out schedule, make a thorough audit of the validity of each invoice. You surely do not want to make these tough times more difficult by overpaying any creditor.

The first thing you must remember is not to try to hide, or avoid phone calls or letters from creditors. The bills will not go away unless you address the problem and design a plan to loosen up the burden. You must level with your creditors, respond to the dunning letters and phone calls and try to make them understand. Vague responses will not satisfy them; but if you assure them of your concerns and good intentions in paying them, they will be to some extent comfortable and more readily willing to cooperate with you.

Your mind will react in a calmer atmosphere to avail you the opportunity of working things out. Now comes the plan for paybacks. First, put together a realistic projection of sales for a period you intend to cover to tie in with a budgeted disbursement schedule.

Based on the above findings of the net difference available will determine what commitments you will be in a position to make to your creditors. Before projecting the figure for pay-outs, consider the monies needed for ongoing inventory since your credit limits will be drastically affected.

Sound business judgment would dictate several projections for short term -- possibly one month; then six months; and another for one year. Together with the knowledge of your liquidity, it is now time for you to contact each creditor -- preferably by phone -- to discuss a plan to dispose of your credit balance. Use your best skills to make your deal with each one individually. Your aim is to pay every vendor as little as possible -- over an extended period of time. The bottom line is your suppliers should be comfortable and it should be within the limits of affordability for you. Include in every discussion the importance of their continuing to ship to you -- hopefully on extended credit -- because of their constant faith in you lies the ability of your sustenance. You will lose many, but the larger percentage you obtain will gain for you more working capital and a direct affect on your comeback.

Rate and classify all creditors as to their importance and significance to the continuance of shipping and service for the preservation of your business.

Consideration should be given as to their willingness to work with you; their size and your ability to negotiate a small settlement for outstanding bills; amount owed each company; and their interest in future shipments.

There are basically three areas which you should pursue to satisfy arrangements to meet the expectations of each of your creditors. Each offer should be dealt with according to the individual reaction.

The first way is to suggest a percentage of the amount due to be paid every month -- a good figure would be ten percent. Secondly, you might consider asking for a twenty-four month consideration. Thirdly, you might offer the entire payment within thirty days, if a considerable discount is given (50%, 40%, 30%). Many creditors could readily agree to this large cut because they might feel that the risk is getting too great with your account and one half or a percentage of the loaf is better than none.

Keep in mind that your offering must be based on the portion of monies left after evaluating cash flow needs for continued inventory "to keep the fire burning". Your goal in a pay-out schedule is to stretch your dollars as far as they will go.

I operated a successful business for many years, always handling my obligations on a very current basis. After a large expansion which didn't prove favorable, I found my company was running into a cash flow problem.

I had to help solve the situation to "stop the bleeding". The first thing I did was to realistically project my company's sales for one full year. I then calculated all expenses of the operation, including new purchases, which would be on a current basis. Then finally I figured the balance to be used for pay-backs of bills in arrears.

After close scrutinization, I came to the conclusion that I could be comfortable with enough remaining funds that would allow me a ten percent reimbursement on a monthly basis for each aged invoice.

The next move was to contact each of my approximately two hundred creditors that I had "good news and bad news". I wrote or called each and told them of my economic crisis and said the good news was that I had a plan to pay everything in arrears in full -- but the bad news was that it would take almost a year to accomplish my righteous intentions. Some hassled me, but the majority were very understanding and cooperative -- even to the point of continuing shipping merchandise on a special arrangement.

Now, the key was to devise a system which accomplished my purpose. I designed a large spreadsheet with multiple columns. Each line at the top had a weekly date and there were a total of twenty across -- enough for over a third of the year. The first column listed each creditor with forty lines down, while the second listed the full amount due. Five of these sheets were done to cover all the debts and three sheets for a group.

I was ready to fill in the total amounts due for each account. To make it work, the starting payments were promised on alternating weeks during the monthly period. The first commitment of ten percent was then written in pencil for every creditor, dividing all those who were due money into four groups over the month and the total of each week equalled ten percent of the anticipated surplus. After the reimbursement was made, my bookkeeper circled the amount. If as in later months a pay-out was detained or squeezed into the next week, it would be erased and placed into the fifth week. Overall there were few revisions and through the year my entire indebtedness was cleared up.

The strength behind my program was consistency, being firm with those that were vocal and living up to my commitments. The spreadsheet project was attainable and the end result was extremely successful. My creditors gained renewed respect and confidence because I lived up to my promises. My suppliers again felt comfortable shipping to my company.

If your business deals with receivables, be sure to draw up a strong and practical plan to make every attempt to receive monies due you -- even if small settlements must be made. This, of course, further strengthens your ability to clear up your payables.

Strategies that Worked in My Business

In this chapter I have detailed my one experience working up the "Pay-Out Schedule." I will now describe further the guts, perseverance, tenacity and even frustration it took to keep this plan alive and doable both from the creditors' aspects as well as my own.

Let's analyze both sides -- my company and the creditors. From my view, it was a do or die situation. It acted as a necessary tool to clear my debts, build up a positive cash flow rather than a negative balance, and to increase monies for on-going expenses, supplies and merchandise.

The creditors' prime interest was to get paid for services or merchandise delivered -- as soon as possible with as much compensation. Realizing the financial predicament I was in put them into a "take it or leave it position." At first, their reaction was disappointment, then anger, and then the realization of cooperation.

The idea of personally talking on the phone, if possible, to each person of authority of every company with outstanding bills proved to be the key to their support and participation. It demonstrated good faith and credibility.

It was no easy task for my company to live up to exactly the timing of the spreadsheets and commitments, but the variations and changes along the way was probably less than they expected. Many of the creditors would be on the phone to me in just a few days after the checks were to be received --

and this, of course, created pressure and required patience on my part to explain. I did try in most instances to call those with late payments before they phoned me. This, no doubt, was appreciated but also, at times others made it tough and discouraging.

Overall, it worked extremely well and the entire project accomplished what I needed for survival -- time, working capital and, ultimately, creditor support.

Lessons Learned

- *Pacify creditors with a detailed plan for prolonging payments.*
- *Face the situation openly and seek their cooperation and support.*
- *Do not hesitate to attempt obtaining partial settlements.*
- *Live up to all commitments.*

SAMPLE OF PAY-OUT SCHEDULE AT 10% MONTHLY

Projected Dates to be Paid

Creditors	Total Amount Due	5/1	5/8	5/15	5/22	5/29	6/5	6/12	6/19	6/26	7/3	7/10	7/17
Creditor #1	$1620.00	162				162				162			
Creditor #2	$15,840		1584				1584				1584		
Creditor #3	$7,216			721				721				721	
Creditor #4	$347				34				34				34
Creditor #5	$2,110			211				211				211	
Creditor #6	$10,150				1015				1015				1015
Creditor #7	6287		628				628				628		

SUPPLIER AND CREDITOR REPAYMENT PLAN

SUPPLIER AND CREDITOR	TOTAL DUE	PAST DUE AMOUNT	# DAYS PAST DUE	NEW MONTHLY PAYMENT	# EXCESS PAYMENTS REQUIRED	EXCESS CASH GENERATED

(continued)

SUPPLIER AND CREDITOR REPAYMENT PLAN

SUPPLIER AND CREDITOR	TOTAL DUE	PAST DUE AMOUNT	# DAYS PAST DUE	NEW MONTHLY PAYMENT	# EXCESS PAYMENTS REQUIRED	EXCESS CASH GENERATED
TOTALS:						

Agreement to Adjust Debt

FOR GOOD AND VALUABLE CONSIDERATION AND ONE DOLLAR, the undersigned as a creditor of _____ (Debtor) hereby enters into this agreement to reduce the indebtedness due the undersigned on the following terms and conditions:

1. The Debtor and the Creditor agree that the present amount due and owing is $_____.

2. The Debtor and Creditor agree that the Creditor shall accept $_____ as full and total payment on said debt in complete discharge and settlement of all amounts due, however the accepted amount herein shall be fully and punctually paid.

3. If the Debtor fails to fully pay the reduced accepted amount, the creditor shall have full rights to prosecute the claim for the original debt due less any payments made by Debtor.

4. If the Debtor defaults payments by more than 10 days, he/she agrees to pay all reasonable attorneys' fees and costs of collection.

5. This agreement shall be binding upon the benefit of the Debtor and Creditor, their successors, assigns, representatives or executors.

_____ _____ _____ _____(SEAL)
Witness   Date   Debtor   Date

_____ _____ _____ _____(SEAL)
       Witness   Date   Debtor   Date

Agreement to Extend the Time for Payment of Debt

FOR VALUE RECEIVED,

_____ (Creditor)
and
_____(Debtor),
undersigned, hereby acknowledge and agree that:

1. The sum of $_____, presently due and payable, to the Creditor but the Debtor is unable to fully pay same at present.

2. In further consideration of the amount due to the Creditor, the Debtor agrees to extend the time for payment of said debt under the following terms:

3. If the Debtor fails to make any payments in a timely manner as agreed on the extended time for payment, the Creditor shall have full rights to proceed for the collection of the entire balance then remaining.

4. If the Debtor defaults in payment, it shall be the responsibility of the Debtor to pay all reasonable attorneys' fees and costs of collection.

5. This agreement shall be binding upon the benefit of the Debtor and Creditor, their successors, assigns, representatives or executors.

_____ _____ _____ _____(SEAL)
Witness   Date   Debtor   Date

_____ _____ _____ _____(SEAL)
Witness   Date   Debtor   Date

Leon Albin

Promissory Note

FOR VALUE RECEIVED, the undersigned jointly and promise to pay to the order of _____
the sum of _____ ($_____)
Dollars, together with interest thereon at the rate of
_____% per annum on any unpaid balance.

The above sum, with interest, shall be paid in _____ installments of $_____ each, with a first payment due _____, _____, and the same amount on the same day of each thereafter until the full amount of principal and accrued interest is paid in full. All payments shall be first applied to earned interest with the balance to the principal. The undersigned may make pre-pay this Note in whole or in part without any penalty.

This Note shall be fully payable upon demand of any holder in the event the undersigned shall default in making any payments due under this Note 10 days after its due date.

In the event of any default, the undersigned agree to pay all reasonable attorneys' fees and costs of collection to the extent permitted by law. All parties to this Note agree to remain fully bound notwithstanding any extension, modification or release or discharge of any party or collateral under this Note.

_____ _____ _____ _____(SEAL)
Witness   Date   Debtor   Date

_____ _____ _____ _____(SEAL)
Witness   Date   Debtor   Date

Extension of Agreement

Extension of Agreement made by _____

and _____.

    This Agreement expires on _____, _____, and the parties desire to extend and continue same, provided that said Agreement shall be extended for an additional term commencing upon the expiration of the original term and expiring on _____, _____.

    This extension shall be on the same terms and conditions as contained in the original Agreement except as for additional changes herewith.

    The extension of Agremeent shall be binding upon benefit of the parties, their successors and assigns and executors.

_____ _____ _____ _____(SEAL)
Witness   Date   Debtor   Date

_____ _____ _____ _____(SEAL)
Witness   Date   Debtor   Date

CHAPTER 9

Don't Be Intimated By Creditors

Prelude

Creditors will start the "squeeze" when they sense your financial setback. Many will be quick to forget the loyal and valuable customer you were and will put the pressure on for late payments. You must exert strength not to be intimidated by their threats. You must be responsive to assure them of your honest objectives.

Although some creditors will cooperate with good faith intentions for pay-outs, others will react differently when they get insight regarding financial set-backs or tighter cash flow. All want to get paid for merchandise shipped or services rendered, but the approaches as to your problems or collection are different.

Too few remember and appreciate the years of business and profit you afforded them. Many couldn't care less about yesterday, the present or the future. They only see the possible loss of dollars and will treat you coldly, indifferently, and unconcerned. They will worry you by phone or in the mail with threats of collectors, attorneys and suits.

Then there are those who do not forget the valuable customer you have been and will do everything in tough times to show their appreciation. They will show compassion and understanding and try to help you get out of your dilemma. They will indicate their willingness to work out a plan of payment and even promise continued shipment of merchandise to help your survival.

Whatever approach is taken by the creditors, do not get alarmed so as to use all your mental and physical abilities to work yourself out of your situation. You must be able to listen and respond; but be sure you do not make commitments you will be unable to keep.

Do not give false promises and if the answers aren't available when you get a call or letter, tell them you'll get back to them by a certain date. Always be sure to live up to your obligation. Do not ignore; the bill won't go away.

Don't be intimidated by screaming or threats. Attempt to make the creditors understand that you are trying your best. Explain to them what you are doing to better the situation in order to make funds available for payments.

Try to pacify and keep your creditors calm and comfortable by impressing them of your understanding. Above all, maintain your composure.

Be assured that everything won't run smooth with your creditors when you offer a pay-out schedule, or when you ask for concessions off the regular terms or late invoices. The phones will be ringing off the hook and the mail will get heavier. Some will go as far as threats to turn over your account to a collection agency or an attorney.

Do not bend from your proposals, which was obviously worked out based on your cash flow or projections. Any commitments you make will be expected by your creditors in a timely fashion. Their reaction later to an unfulfilled promise will anger them much more than the original contact.

Since you should realize that you can't avoid your creditors contacting you when you are in arrears of payments, it always works in your favor if you call them first. A short phone call to a person with responsibility will go a long way to giving you extension of time or a longer range of payment.

Personal conversation or a meeting is much appreciated and in most cases will ease the burden of pressure. It is to everyone's advantage and makes good business sense to have a better understanding and have a meeting of the minds.

Always be up front and face the problem in a realistic manner. Talk openly, honestly and fairly. Let them know you have candid objectives and try to make yourself worthy of their confidence.

The important thing about payable concessions is that everybody becomes comfortable and it serves a definite purpose for both the creditor and the business.

The creditors are agreeable because it gives them a reassurance that not only is there an intent for payment, but a time period to expect their monies. Also, it gives them new life not to lose a customer for future profits.

The business is content because it loosens up additional cash flow and gives hope and life for continuance and survival.

Financial institutions will generally be more callous and will want to see hard facts of your position. Before you meet with them, have your accountant put together some data to handle the situation. Projections for the future can show up better than the past.

It is in your hands to sound and look confident with the skill and stamina to talk it out. Be courageous and compelled and you will marvel at yourself and your ability to get their support.

Strategies that Worked in My Business

It is ironic how a supplier can turn so fast from friend to foe. Creditors forget too quickly the many good years and all the profitable dollars earned from a loyal and faithful customer. Those were the "good ole days" when all they needed was an automatic phone call or visit for an order. But now they have to take the bitter with the sweet, and it is tough to accept.

I remember so clearly the harassment and threats from several when the payments were slower than what they were accustomed to. When you are thrown into the water, you either sink or swim, and I learned rapidly that I was going to keep my head above the dangerous level. I was determined not to let them drag me down. I felt I was due a fair shake with reasonable understanding and cooperation.

Immediately upon getting into this dilemma, I sought out a bankruptcy attorney who specialized in collections and court action. I retained a lawyer who had one of the top reputations and followings in my area for collection of delinquent accounts, whose clients were mostly creditors. By me tying him up meant that those seeking to collect from my company had to use other legal assistance who were not as reputable and aggressive, since, of course, he couldn't handle both sides. He quickly taught me my rights and responses to threats and how to react. We both worked well together and became fearless.

In one instance, a creditor's attorney called and said that if he didn't get paid within five days, he was going across the street from his office and put me into bankruptcy. This sounded frightening and I immediately called my lawyer who said to forget that type of call. No one can act that fast.

Another time, the executive vice president of my largest supplier, who through the previous fifteen years had sold me $3,000,000 worth of merchandise, came into my office. He sat across from my desk, sternly stared at me, said "We must be paid at once," then handed me a statement of $139,000. I then looked at him straight in the eye and boldly said, "Here, do you want my keys?" He was stunned, glanced at me and said, "Please pay as soon as you can," got up and walked out.

Not being alarmed or terrified, but genuinely concerned allowed me to be self assured and confident to act and respond in an appropriate and relaxed manner. I got out of this mess without one suit or judgment against me or my company.

Lessons Learned

- *Remain cool and calm and don't over-react.*
- *Earn your creditors' respect and confidence.*
- *Don't be frightened or intimidated by their threats and pressure.*
- *Face up to your financial problems.*

CHAPTER 10

Re-evaluate Profitability

Prelude

> *Profit represents the backbone of a successful business. Each facet of your operations plays an integral part for staying in the black. Improved management, tighter authority and better cash control methods will bring about more profit.*

The bottom line for business survival and for progress is profit. There are many factors and components that "spell" profitability.

Profitability is an important part of the survival equation. In order to produce a profit, you must speculate with variations; generally the higher the risk, the higher the cost, the higher the profit. Gains are a necessary share of the system.

Business is a science regulated by people; controlled by certain factors consisting of economy changes; in market concepts; and dependent on its progress by proper management to produce earnings.

Let's go back to the days before the business began and it was just a dream. Many thoughts and ideas were "thrown around" on working to put it together. If you stop and think and remember how much effort went into the very start, you again will appreciate all the details, the planning and the strategy. You will recall how careful you were and how frugal you had to be with dollars available. Then you went forward to blend all the parts and put the package together and bring in the right people to make it happen.

You went through the original obstacle and were successful for this hurdle and spent years operating your business and obviously earning a profit. "When the going gets tough -- the tough get going" -- and this is when a full re-evaluation is necessary.

Somewhere down the line tactics for profitability must have gone astray. Since surplus represents the net difference of income and expenses, let's revisit all the components that make up this balance. The income, of course, must be high enough to cover all the expenses to generate any yield -- which simply means that it is imperative to get the income up and the expenses down. Controlling projected and actual monies that come in and commitments for expenditures is a major part of the profit and loss process.

It is very simple: work on both at the same time; but there is no question that cutting expenses is quicker to accomplish. Start immediately to cut off all the "fat". Look hard at personnel who are not fully productive and be firm and strong to make a change, combine or eliminate the position. This cutback or tightening up will help at once. Merging positions is an old "trick" and giving additional responsibilities to employees generally gives incentives and builds morale -- especially when additional compensation is given. When times are rough, the increase in salary even with additional duties is not always necessary. A detailed evaluation process will provide a thorough area of expertise.

Next, examine every expense on the operational statement and study very carefully where it can be cut down or fully eliminated. Put your best foot forward and bear down hard because this is the real key to improving your circumstances. Cover every item and pick your brain how each one individually can be handled. Cut as much as possible, or at least try to decrease even a small percentage as you go down the list. After you have done as much as you thought you could do, thoroughly review once more to reduce even further.

Following your own study, call in some key personnel to evaluate with you. There can be many dollars they feel can still be eliminated after you sliced to the limit. Then, the final stage of this ordeal should be to meet, phone or write each supplier of these expenses to get their cooperation in lowering costs.

While your disbursements and controls regulate your outlay of monies, your products and services are two segments which create the income. Both work hand in hand with sound management organization and operation.

To build and maintain the income and services, you must buy and merchandise to meet and beat your competition; have a good product mix; display your stock in a saleable manner; create a good market for your products; generate a worthy image; build an acceptance and responsiveness from your customers; and above all, produce a firm, loyal and conscientious employee group to accomplish all of the above.

Simultaneously, explore all methods of increasing sales or service to build income. Start with current products to promote sales. Follow closely tie-in items that would be conclusive for seasonal purchases. Watch for holiday specialties and plan displays and emphasis for these occasions of the year.

Your income and sales is directly attributable to the proper valuation of your inventory.

Following are suggestions to help pricing your merchandise to make a profit:

- Check your competition.

- Mark-up your merchandise according to the value and supply and demand.

- Each product should stand on its own.

- Keep a uniform and set price.

- Create a policy for volume users as to percentage of discount to be offered.

- Do not hesitate to reduce or sell below cost if item is "sitting on the shelf".

- Your overall profit structure is based on all merchandise, so price some items higher and some lower, depending on sound merchandising.

- Determine products that are recognized lost leaders.

- Evaluate items which are faster turnover and always maintain adequate back-up inventory.

- Determine your high and low selling price acceptable to your customers.

- Follow seasonal timing for appropriate sales.

- Always watch competitors' advertising.

Moving departments around the store gives the appearance and effect of a new look and generates customer interest. Always be sure that the departments are stocked full with all related items displayed within the same area. Multiple offerings stimulate higher unit sales as well as items sold in conjunction with others.

Your promotional strengths play a big part in conveying to your customers the values of your merchandise. Advertising with your own money -- and just as important "co-op" dollars by your suppliers -- should give you adequate funds. Study the best media and method of using these promotional funds.

Trading up to a higher priced or better quality is an "old trick" that builds sales and profit. This requires good salespeople to be knowledgeable of the store's inventory. Another important factor is for a sales clerk to be trained in the technique to "spin off" to another clerk a customer who can't be sold -- giving the store a "double shot" at the sale.

Building inventory turnover is an integral part of the profit structure. This represents the number of times in a year the merchandise is turned over. Dividing the cost of goods sold by the average total inventory will give the amount of times it has turned over. A business should strive for as high an inventory turn as possible.

If your products are not moving, your money becomes stagnant and cannot be used for more updated merchandise. Therefore, advertising sales and discounts must be planned to move slow moving stock. Of course, sales are planned to include special purchases with current inventory.

Another ingredient of profit is the mark-up percentage. It is imperative to have sufficient mark-up over your cost to cover all expenses and make a gain.

There are many other unique methods to create increased sales -- and each company must study which ways are successful for them. If one idea doesn't work, study all angles to re-evaluate what is best for you.

Tight controls is the key ingredient to making a profit. It is imperative to keep a strong handle on all areas of your company:

- Cash must be accounted both for incoming and outgoing.
- Be very cautious on extension of credit.
- Have a fool-proof system for goods received.
- Create a bookkeeping and accounts payable system which will closely monitor all payments, so as not to duplicate.

To complete the profit ratio, strong efforts and attention must be concentrated to watch where and how the monies are spent. Assuming you are "buying right" to put the merchandise on the shelves, you should be extremely concerned about the balance of the picture to keep expenses down to a point in order to make a good return to generate cash flow.

Begin with forecasting and budgeting to give you a visual portrait and direction for profitability. Since all steps have been taken in income producing, now the important correlation of accounting and controls is a must. After this valuable information is prepared, be sure to use it regularly as a guide.

Incorporate all the data of a balance sheet, statement of profit and loss, elaborating on each item based on a thorough discussion and projection of each item with the appropriate person or persons within the company.

On the income side, analyze all the factors which will either increase or show a decline for the projected period. Evaluate the market, change of products, competition (new and old) and how the general economy will affect your business.

As to the liabilities, start with fixed expenses, like rent, taxes, licenses, debt repayment, loans and payment for fixtures and equipment, necessary insurance, and depreciation. These obviously have been set; however, all the other variable expenses of salaries, advertising, utilities, distribution, entertainment, etc. must be projected to be affordable.

Your employee relationship and participation is an integral force in making everything happen. Finding the right help has become one of the major problems in operating a business. Do not minimize any efforts to setting up a good interviewing system; explaining the positions; clearly defining your expectations and needs; and fitting them into the jobs based on abilities and skills.

Explain to them your policies, definitive programs on what they can expect from your firm as to starting salaries, promotions, fringe benefits, vacations, and other matters that might arise important to them. Set the stage for a good company/employee relationship so as to encourage contentment, top productivity, and results.

Improved management, tighter operation and better cash control methods will bring about more profit.

Strategies that Worked in My Business

To rebuild profitability, I set up a project of total company participation. Everyone in my association -- from clerks through store managers, supervisors, and buyers -- were given suggestion sheets to share their impressions. Each employee was given one week to present to management his or her thoughts as to what was needed to improve any facet of our organization to increase sales and cut down expenses.

Inviting them to give their opinions and making them feel part of everything worked wonders. They were given the option to send in recommendations anonymously or signed. Their thoughts ranged from criticizing the bosses to evaluating every phase of our entire operation. They covered types of merchandise, methods of distribution, employee loyalty and dishonesty, improving customer relations and cutting expenses.

- There were many accepted recommendations on changing of merchandise -- more conducive and individualized to the respective areas -- rather than similar items in all stores.
- They were more cognizant of the competition -- not to be undersold.
- I was given tips on wasted steps of merchandise distribution.

- I found out about unfaithful and unproductive employees.

- Store clerks voiced their cooperation to cut down help during slower periods.

The open door policy encouraged and boosted better employee relations. The team action paid off as everyone felt he and she played a part to begin reconstruction of a stronger position for our company.

Lessons Learned

- *Look back to your beginnings and rediscover the strengths that make you profitable and successful.*

- *Simplify how you do business.*

- *Do processes add value?*

- *Trim excess weight.*

- *Is pricing consistent with what you offer customers?*

- *How are you positioned vs. competition?*

CHAPTER 11

Be a Bull on Operations

Prelude

> *"When the going gets tough, the tough get going" -- and that's the time to secure your belt. That is when a company must follow the critical signs and take a new look as to what is needed to strengthen its operation. Immediate action must be taken for efficient leadership and instant cutbacks.*

Survival in business means tightening up your belt when times get tough and a declining economy is faced with a recession or depression. As soon as the vital signs flash out, a company must take that warning and begin to study what can be done to improve its operation. The earlier you jump in to appraise your situation, the better opportunity you present for hanging in during these changing times. Take a hard nose approach to survive by reducing costs and cutting back.

Suppliers and creditors respect the business that protects its interest. They gain confidence when they see you are helping with your own troubles. You can still be courteous and fair while doing the job of being a good businessman. Doing everything it takes to change your company during these trying days is the difference of survival or failure. Do not hesitate to show that you realize what has to be done.

The immediate salvation of a business during a drop in the economy is better management, tighter controls, and instant reductions. Being as tough as it takes to get it done is the pattern you must follow. Living off the "fat of the land" is history, and facing the drought must be accomplished in its fullest. Pulling in your horns will bring about terminations, changes of responsibilities and duties and salary decreases. Strong marketing strategies and analysis are necessary for any up-surge. Until you make it happen, be assured of its seriousness and that things can get worse.

Concentrate on curtailing costs in every department -- with no exceptions. Review every detail and use of your facilities, equipment, and stock. Evaluate performance of everyone connected with your organization -- whether it be management, employees, your professionals, outside contractors, or suppliers.

Your review will give you ideas of systems you can change or where to tighten up when necessary. Encourage suggestions from everyone to participate in cutting back.

After you have evaluated everybody, study yourself, and be objective as to how you can improve and use your time and money more wisely. Putting it all together, you will be surprised the dollars available for you to save.

Downgrading costs will immediately upgrade your struggle to survive.

Diminishing overhead is the most important project that must be done to create a cash flow. Every dollar must be scrutinized in your company. Wherein prior to this point many items and luxuries were bought, now your spending habits must be very frugal. Every expenditure must be counted as a very necessary item and eliminated if possible.

Strive for a large percentage reduction. Every person in the organization must be accountable and taught and impressed of the importance of cooperating in this project. Study each department and keep pressing the managers to stay on top of their employees. This is a team effort.

Terminating employees is a difficult chore for management -- but is a must if the situation presents itself. By all means, dishonesty or disloyalty cannot be tolerated, but also a hard look must be considered in severance, if cutbacks are necessary for reducing expenses.

Flexible expenses must be looked at constantly like automobile usage, entertainment, maintenance telephones and many other applicable in your business.

The foremost concern is to better your condition and build up its financial position. You must recoup losses and get back

on your feet to raise cash by saving within the company --
while making every attempt to increase sales. It will take
determination and fortitude to reduce costs, duplication and
waste -- but if this is what must be done to put the business on
stabilized grounds, don't hesitate to begin immediately.

The effects of your efforts will catch on quickly. Employees
within your organization will start reacting favorably and will
join in to make it happen. Your suppliers and creditors will
gain added respect knowing that you are making an attempt
to tighten up during trying times -- and you will get a big
boost in having your reductions reach its potential.

The average business person spends more dollars in
managing his or her firm when things are running normal.
There are times when letting the guard down is costly -- but
hardly harmful when there is no crunch. However, the fringes
and the perks must be a thing of the past when the chips are
down.

Cutting as much expenses as possible becomes a reality and necessity when you are faced with tightening up the operation. Don't worry about going overboard to reach the happy medium, and be sure to include everyone to participate. The entire organization must be accountable and realize the importance of an all-out endeavor. Don't criticize or dwell on the past -- but impress each employee of the project for the future.

After trimming down each cost where you feel there is no more to cut, turn to the big chore of eliminating major parts of your company. Consolidate and merge together different departments and locations. Joining forces is the best way to reduce all overhead, decreasing all areas of expenses.

In a retail chain, the closing of a non-profitable store creates profit for the company and strengthens the balance of the business with stronger personnel and a more concise operation.

Space is costly and utilizing every square foot of selling and storage areas will bring a return of dollars. My chain of stores for many years received distribution of merchandise through our large warehouse. This required huge personnel and mass inventories. One day I came upon the thought of restructuring the basement of one of my larger locations for use as the warehouse center, utilizing similar conveyors, shelving and activities as the older warehouse. The plan worked well, selling the warehouse building for a very large sum of money and saving many thousands of dollars for many years in utilizing my revamped distribution center.

There were several occasions when I saw the need of consolidating and cutting back by shorter business hours and closing stores when the sales didn't warrant its expenses and the return was insufficient to compensate for the extended times. Shortening hours conserved many dollars in salaries and heat, light and power. Complete closings saved rent as well as inventory and the consolidation of stores to smaller space accounted for extra dollars.

It would be timely to give a good hard look at controlling shrinkage.

Relating and recognizing this disturbing information makes it a necessity that you have concern. There is no business that is immune from this most severe problem. Statistics show that 50% of all people are outright dishonest. Twenty-five percent are on the border and 25% are honest. These astonishing figures make it mandatory to make it a priority to hire honest people, and to place controls which you can be comfortable.

Qualities of Courage Needed for Survival

- Create the challenge to proceed
- Believe in yourself
- Be involved and determined

- Build a group around you

- Know what is happening in your area

- Ability to exchange views and ideas with others

- Don't hesitate to take action and make changes

- Build confidence and esteem with everyone you have

  contact

- Gain your community respect.

Cutting down the overhead can't be emphasized too strongly when all efforts are pointed toward survival. Sometimes you can't see the forest for the trees, so chopping down some of the wood will give a clearer view.

Giving a second and a third look as to expenditures in a business will surprise even the most perceptive individual. When things are in place, they become habit forming and change doesn't come too easily. You must be motivated and know it is a top priority to cut back. Pushing yourself to look and examine each and every disbursement is a chore that demands full attention.

Overhead consists of fixed and variable expenses. Obviously, not too much can be done with fixed expenses -- but they do deserve attention. For instance, rent is set, either on a monthly basis or a lease. However, it is always worth a try to talk to the landlord and explain your circumstances. If an agreement cannot be reached to reduce the payments, then possibly a reduction in space can be done with the fees being lessened accordingly.

Another fixed expense (unless on a percentage basis) is salaries. Start first by looking at your own in tough times. If you can live on less -- now is the time to do it. The owner/owners and stockholders should personally adhere to a no salary draw while working toward eliminating operational costs. Then review everyone else's salary and try to impress certain individuals that cutbacks must be necessary to survive. Promise full consideration when you are over the hurdle. When occasions present themselves, salaries must be merged with employees assuming additional duties and responsibilities. Unfortunately, there could be unemployment for some -- but tightening up is the sign of the times.

An example illustrating cutting back an organization to reduce overhead can be found in my chain. There were two losing locations. Both stores had two to three years remaining on the expiration of the leases. Each day while these stores were opened they consumed expenses of rent, salaries, heat, light, power, telephone, delivery and supervisory services as well as each store carrying over $75,000 in inventory at cost.

In order to be able to close these sites, I had to negotiate with the landlords on a settlement to vacate. We finally agreed on a six month rental figure, one amounting to $14,000 and the other $15,000. My company accordingly saved thousands of dollars (despite the payments of rent) on the various operating expenses in addition to about $150,000 in merchandise which fit very nicely into my other stores. Additionally, we gained by eliminating unnecessary help by transferring key and capable employees to strengthen other parts of our chain.

Cutting variable expenses is an easier task. There could be areas that you can do without; or there can be chores you are "farming out" that should be merged back into your own operation. Carefully reviewing every disbursement will surely bring results. Changing routines, habits and methods can save money.

Payroll is the highest variable expense in a company. A review should be made how to decrease in this area without affecting or diminishing the needs of the business. There are several methods to accomplish this.

Wherever possible, change from the conventional manner of fixed hourly or weekly salaries to a commission bonus or incentive plan. You might find it practical to combine certain jobs or probably less hours per week for certain positions.

All employees must be impressed to keep the fire burning lower in every area. Remember every dollar saved is a dollar earned.

Biting the bullet and eliminating everything possible will make you the bull that is necessary to clean up your operation and improve your financial situation. In the long run this action will make your business stronger and lasting.

Strategies that Worked in My Business

Waste has always been bothersome to me -- so emphasis on reviewing and evaluating expenses was right up my alley. The quickest and most effective way to reduce operating costs was to throw them into the hands of the "troops." I proved to myself that giving them the responsibility to help make decisions worked.

I set up a contest with a monthly bonus of $200.00 to each store manager (his or her choice for self or to be divided) who showed the highest percentage cut. A form was sent out each month to all store managers listing each variable expense of the same month for the previous year, showing dollars and percentages to total sales. The chart allowed space for the office to fill in after the end of the month showing results, reflecting the individual and overall operational expense. The store who produced the best total percentage savings for the month was the winner.

This in-house competition ran for twelve months and saved our company thousands of dollars. Not only did it prove successful for the time it ran, but became habit forming, and the reduction in expenses continued thereafter with similar expectations and performance.

Month of _____

Expense	Previous Year Dollar Expenditure	Previous Year % to Sales	Current Year Dollar Expenditure	Current Year % to Sales	Net Difference

(continued)

Expense	Previous Year Dollar Expenditure	Previous Year % to Sales	Current Year Dollar Expenditure	Current Year % to Sales	Net Difference

THE BALL IS IN YOUR COURT
$200 Monthly Bonus for Best Store Performance

Lessons Learned

- *Intensify your efforts to diminish operational functions.*

- *Key is better management, tighter controls, and instant cutbacks.*

- *Take a hard look at variable expenses.*

- *Utilize all skills to build sales.*

CHAPTER 12

Tighten Up Lines and Seek New Products

Prelude

This takes real ingenuity to make changes in your merchandising. Cutting down on similar items and making room for new products and ideas will help your cash flow. Reducing your variety will help your turnover, lowering your cash input to inventory. That will avail you more dollars to be creative to open up new markets.

Spreading merchandise thinner has the biggest impact on investment -- but there has to be a lot of thought as to what to eliminate; so as not to affect sales and cash flow. The old adage "you can't do business on an empty wagon" could be a reality if you don't concentrate on sound merchandising techniques when curtailing the selection.

Duplicated lines of different suppliers, similar items and articles that have like detail should be sold off as soon as possible and not reordered. Variations of sizes and shapes can be omitted as well as secondary colors which are not popular.

In other words, deep thought must be given to each item and every line to get rid of slower items, dead stock and in general slower turnover inventory. This could make it more difficult to trade up; but offset with more concentrated training, stronger efforts, giving more attention to customers' needs, and changed attitudes can produce the difference in a successful project of thinning the lines.

Reducing the variety and keeping close observation on the depth will help your turnover of merchandise which will accomplish its true purpose.

To revitalize more life into the company, a new approach must be taken so as to stimulate profits, cash flow, and strengthen the business.

Being creative on your own is not enough. Don't hesitate to search the competition to seek out new ideas to enhance your business. There is absolutely nothing unethical about looking at others to put together new concepts. Study change of trends and fashion habits.

Researching related businesses, other operations which are not similar, competition and trade shows will open up your eyes to products which are being distributed in your areas as well as other markets. Product development can be enhanced with the assistance and interest of your salespeople, suppliers and customers. An evaluation of this study will help you decide which items you feel can be merchandised in conjunction with the lines and items you presently carry.

Consideration for additional inventory must be based on creativity of traffic and profit. It makes good sense to work on a closer margin if it generates volume. Of course, items which produce less traffic should demand a larger profit. Above all, be careful not to create a further cash flow crunch with dead stock.

Another method of revitalization is opening up new markets for your products. Expanding your consumer territory will extend potential to your company without investing exhorbitant dollars to cover these new areas. Continuing with your same inventory base with more frequent turnover will allow you to watch any new dollars needed. You must, however, be cognizant of control of additional operational costs -- so as not to cut the profit picture.

If you can use current manpower to spread themselves thinner and accomplish this new development with little added expense, you will open up additional revenues never realized.

Trading on improved products and markets will not only build innovative ideas from your personnel; it will also bolster the morale and enthusiasm of everyone around you.

Strategies that Worked in My Business

After the transition from our outdoor image to full line sporting goods stores and closely scrutinizing the merchandise we then carried, I realized that there were several lines carried which had to be dropped or drastically reduced in inventory. Although most of everything in our stores reflected customers we catered to, we found the new patterns and change-over were very significant in adopting new items, diminishing emphasis on others.

Products that previously were very meaningful to our overall sales were now projected to be of lesser importance. Decisions had to be made for their full elimination or some reduction.

The fishing and hunting departments comprised approximately twenty percent of our total volume; consumed about thirty percent of our inventory dollars; the margins were closer than other lines; absorbed considerable time in shopping the markets. Accordingly, I made the appropriate decision to close-out these departments.

We continued in the direction of sporting goods rather than the leisure field. Previously, we had been very extensive in camping, carrying not only the basic lines, but inventoried many extended and related items. These were also dropped.

Further, we picked up more depth in active apparel and equipment which fit in the thousands of inventory dollars. It not only allowed us more money to spend in our new direction, but rejuvenated our updated conception.

Lessons Learned

- *Develop your abilities to be a keen merchandiser.*
- *Curtail lines, develop faster turnover without jeopardizing sales volume.*
- *Use your ingenuity to enhance your products.*

CHAPTER 13

Value of Your Employees

Prelude

Your team represents your support, and their loyalty and ability can make the difference for your business continuance. Each employee must be a contributing part. Their attitudes and efficiency are directly responsible for the performance of your company. You must analyze these strengths and weaknesses to obtain best results.

Employees can make or break a business. These are the direct contacts representing you to the public. The right attitude and enthusiasm go far to building up the image of the company. The customer is immediately impressed with the sales clerk who is knowledgeable and willing to help. Service is too frequently lacking to the public.

Those workers who have earned the right for their positions are the only ones who should be carried on the payroll. All others should be replaced or dropped. Those not adding to your company's success are a big factor in the internal problems. The day of reckoning has come and each person's value must be looked at.

Befitting habits and disposition are directly related to attitudes and conduct -- feelings, composure, outlook of goals, patience and ability to handle pressures and responsibilities. Also affected would be employee's panic, confidence and tolerance.

Appropriate behavior is imperative and you can't be tolerant of insincerity or uncaring people. They must know why they are there and the contributions they make to the company's sustenance. Be specific and thorough in your description and explanation of each job, and motivate all personnel to give top performances. Good working conditions must be part of your agenda and you should encourage participation, suggestions and new ideas. Make them feel how essential their input is to the final decision makings.

The basic reason for employment is the compensation or salary received for payment of your work. However, incentives and perks, environment, duties, responsibilities, fellow employees and management are all considerations for contentment.

The head of the business cannot achieve success in the turnaround project without his/her entire team of people using exerted efforts and ingenuity. He/she cannot tolerate anything but full support and coperation and there is no room in his/her company for incompetency or dishonesty.

In the best of times, a company cannot allow internal theft. But when a business is shaky with other problems, a leaking situation could bring on a hastened downfall, and can be the key reason for a final disaster.

People who are insecure with their jobs, have no interest in their position, or have low morale, are prime candidates for dishonesty. Especially when they sense problems in the business, employees are dangerously vulnerable for their changing of good behavior to indecent habits.

Action must be taken immediately at the first detection or suspicion, and this requires precedence over all other chores. Firstly, impress every worker as to the importance of honesty and sincerity. Everyone should be told how imperative it is to help management deter fraudulence. Additional steps must be taken for prevention and stricter controls.

An integral segment of your organization is your employees. They must sense their importance to the operation, as their support and faithfulness to your company will provide you with the tools to continue. They must feel they are part and parcel of what makes everything click.

In today's competitive arena for the best personnel, you must, in addition to fair pay, develop programs for incentives, bonuses or commissions, profit sharing, pensions and health plans. Design the approach which would be adaptable and affordable to your company -- but give ample thought to whatever is practical and acceptable.

Delegate responsibilities in your company -- but keep them as simple as possible. Place emphasis on middle management to help things move and progress.

Since employees are the backbone to a successful organization, develop strong procedures, applications, and interviews to hire those who will best be suited to fill the positions needed. Develop a good technique to hire the most qualified people. Save future waste of time and money.

It can be very cost-effective and productive to seek seniors, part-timers, and handicapped persons who can perform necessary tasks. All newcomers and even veterans need attention as to training and updated methods. Evaluate the limited hours that these prospects can give to your company and question closely if they can meet your requirements and hours.

Before setting up the interview process for hiring, prepare for yourself and those responsible to talk to applicants a pro-forms as to what the needs are: type of people to fill those vacancies and a job description of the duties. In addition to your assessing the prospects, they deserve information about your company and what they can expect from you. This will be a good start to have the appropriate "chemistry".

The interviewing process should be done very thoroughly. Study the application and resume closely to determine the applicant's skills and stability in order to target your needs. Job-hoppers are not people you can build on. Look to those who have a history of long-term employment. New graduates deserve a different type of discussion to determine their basic interest and seriousness to fill your needs. Candidates should be interviewed in a relaxed atmosphere.

Small business employees have a different outlook and expectations than those seeking larger or national corporations. They generally seem more comfortable within their environment and face the challenges with a distinctive approach. The closer and tighter organization has a more inviting appeal to them because it gives them the opportunity to be involved with the decision makers and management. They enjoy the "family" atmosphere.

In a small company, put emphasis on good coordinated relationships amongst your employees. These people can work more harmoniously together and survival and progress are deeply dependent on a solid organization.

Employers are impressed with certain traits with prospective employees who seek employment. These distinctions are observed:

Personal impression

Experience

Past history

Knowledge

Aspirations

Inspiration

State of mind

Brilliance

Drive

Company dedication

Working with people

Desire

Maturity

High caliber

Sound mind

Belief in self

Tranquility

Goals

Upstanding person

Talking ability

Writing ability

Vision

Ability to comprehend

Spirit

Vigor

Finesse with people

Physical condition

Convincing

Originality

Happiness

Tactfulness

Direction

Outside salesmen require certain characteristics which blend into special traits:

- Their personality and strengths to community with people are of utmost importance.

- Salesmanship skills require full know how of the merchandise and explaining to the buyers full information of product knowledge

- A good outside salesman applicant should have the ability to sell the buyer merchandise that works well in his/her organization and build confidence of his/her interest and needs.

- A very important attribute is the ability to working with the suppliers, manufacturers and distributors.

- More self motivation is expected from outside salesman than store clerks.

The background and experience and attitude of a sales rep works well to their benefit.

Verification and References for Background Check

1. Length of time of employment

2. Job duties

3. Reliability and work attendance record

4. Honesty

5. Rating of job performance

6. Opinion of work

7. Ability to get along with supervisors

8. Ability to get along with co-workers

9. Employee's extra efforts to make him/her exceptional

10. Any increases or promotions

11. Any outside intervention of work

12. Reason for leaving position

13. Eligibility for re-employment.

Leon Albin

Methods of Building Employee Efficiency

1. Define expectations

2. Encourage employees to feel part of activities

3. Keep employees abreast of ups and downs in business

4. Command respect as leader

5. Every employee must feel important

6. Check employees

7. Commend whenever possible

8. Do not carry excess luggage of employees

9. Do not undermine employees in public

10. Always try to better work habits

11. Be ready to handle all duties

12. Do not hestitate to give negative answers if necessary

13. Present goals to reach

14. No long meetings

15. Find out information of employees who left.

Assuming you do all the right things to keep your business successful, recognize that the key to maintaining a good sound operation are your employees. They are the ones to strengthen or weaken your organization. Allow them to share responsibilities and delegate chores to get more mileage out of their efforts. Motivate them and give all the encouragement possible for better performance.

The attitudes of your personnel many times are directly dependent on the posture of management. Emphasize and build all aspects of team play and stimulate and inspire them to utilize all their ingenuity and abilities. Make them feel important and an essential component.

In order to obtain the best results and productivity from your people, work closely with them to understand what is expected, and establish a better description of their job duties and responsibilities. It will instill more confidence within your company and everyone will benefit. You will build better employees and stimulate their interest.

Strategies that Worked in My Business

My first employee hired in the original store was raised twenty-two years in our company, and many others that followed grew with us. I always tried to make all personnel feel part of a team and learn as much as possible about his or her position.

I took pride in watching individuals develop and mature with us. Most managers were an outgrowth of their beginnings as clerks. In fact, supervisors and buyers through the years were previously managers.

Our problem with good employee relationship in our business surfaced as our "family" scattered with expansion, contacts became more distant, and everyone was more absorbed in day-to-day responsibilities. Then the realization of maintaining positive attitudes and loyalty were part of our daily endeavors. We never underestimated the importance of our employees, and always continued our efforts to retain their dedication, enthusiasm, product knowledge, interest and concerns for customers and our company.

We began monthly supper meetings for managers to update on policies and new merchandise, exchange views for ideas, and discuss general problems. To cover the needs of all personnel, we sustained competitive salaries and started a family health plan.

The new innovations worked well to keep stability in our company for better employee-management relations.

Lessons Learned

- *Understand and realize the importance of your employees.*
- *Develop a legal and conscientious team.*
- *Expect nothing less than full efforts and dedication.*
- *Their endeavors and accomplishments are an integral key to your success.*

CHAPTER 14

Keeping Up the Morale

Prelude

Morale is the "must" ingredient for the employees to put out their best effort. It builds desire and loyalty and brings forth their best performance. Management must do their part to create the atmosphere and interest necessary to instill enthusiasm and dedication.

While the battle is going on to keep the ship afloat, the crew's spirit must be kept sparkling. Without them, there would be no movement and the motor will burn out. You must instill the jest of life and continuously let them know the important part they play in the entire operation. More than ever, they must have the feeling of belonging.

At the same time while your concerns are for the survival of your business, keep up the morale of your team, so that working together you can accomplish all the necessary steps toward a common interest of gaining progress.

There are several components that make up high morale in a company. Factors that build longevity are salary, benefits, working conditions, atmosphere, management attitude, location and the most important is security. All of the above must be part and parcel to achieving and keeping up the proper disposition.

Every facet must be addressed conscientiously and with utmost concern. Each peg should remain in place and stand on its own to totally accomplish the art of best results. Having the entire organization feel they are a significant asset of the team enhances the effort.

Everybody wants the best salary possible for labor, but given their compensation along with the other expectations will generally satisfy most employees. Comparisons with similar jobs should be reviewed as no one wants to be underpaid. Health insurance, pensions and retirement benefits must be weighed by management but the company must take cost into account. In today's market, benefits add a substantial percentage to employee remuneration.

People who toil day in and day out look forward to good working conditions and atmosphere to keep the enthusiasm up, since the environment of your work place is what you constantly see. The management's approach can "make your day", so despite all your trials and tribulations, as the guiding force, do everything possible to have everyone feel all is well. Attitude and leadership are a big phase of building morale. Location also cannot be overlooked because accessibility, transportation and area are important.

Especially during the crisis, employee morale is a major factor. Put more emphasis on them than ever before in being part of the overall efforts. They must be made to feel that their presence and support is most important to the entire team effort and project for resurfacing. They must be encouraged to use all of their ingenuity and expertise in handling of customers and day to day chores.

Proper spirit will automatically build your company's production, sales and service. Your employees will perform better individually and collectively, and increase your efficiency and results.

Motivation is the key to higher confidence and you must strive to reach for the ultimate in employee relationships and potential. Sound management from the top and leading by example will create good temperament.

Employees have the ability to control their behavior and habits on the job, and will have a great influence on people around them.

A good morale tool is to give adequate credit to performance by employees. Recognizing their efforts and participation will help others join in to be part of the team. This is an easy method to instill confidence for higher goals.

Management must be careful about control and manipulation as threats and punishment will not be as workable as self pride.

Employees must feel that their contribution to their jobs are part of the success of the business, and being conscientious has a significant meaning for the company to move ahead.

Businesses must work on improving the basis of motivating employees. Study your organization and lay the groundwork for people in your company to be uplifted and desirous in building teamwork with you. Make them feel part of what is going on. Encourage them to set goals which are attainable to benefit the company and themselves. Enhance conditions so they want to move ahead.

Consideration for Promoting Morale and Motivation

- Accomplishment
- Workplace
- Obligations
- Company leadership
- Progress

- Promotions

- Compensation

- Good working arrangements

- Bosses

- Position

- Job security

Employees would welcome the opportunity to join in with extra efforts in the turnaround project. Include them and delegate additional chores for their added participation. You will marvel at their added work effort and input in their everyday activities without cost.

Delegating additional responsibilities to employees further enhances their conscientious participation and accomplishments.

Management must be ready and willing to accept their suggestions and invite them to analyze the problems and be part of the solution. Planned meetings on an individual basis as well as group meetings with an agenda to include them with their views and participation will be helpful in bringing up their desires to produce.

The unfortunate belief by most employees is that the company is making a lot of money out of their efforts and accordingly feels underpaid. This type of false analysis by empoyees as to the great profits and income derived from their being there leads to unconscientious, limited effort and very often theft.

To counteract the above, the employers should build interest up by the employees with participation in some management decision and be knowledgeable of the operation and merchandising.

Putting all the fragments together also assures sound security. Working toward a future stability and feeling safe in conjunction with current needs adds up to good employee relationship and high morale.

Strategies that Worked in My Business

Team play requires the feeling of working together, and we never stopped this on-going project to keep our people happy. One bad apple can ruin the entire bushel, and accordingly we always attempted to straighten out the difficulty or dismiss the disgruntled person.

In addition to fair compensation, the benefits of health insurance and liberal merchandise discounts, our employees were made to feel appreciated. Our annual family picnic with barbecue food and games always generated comraderie.

It was a known fact in our organization that most managers and top persons were given advancement from within, and this sentiment of achievement was surely a means of encouragement.

We kept the interest of all the employees by sustaining a four page WEEK-LEE newsletter. It consisted of a format which included general company information, merchandising tips, employee of the week, and the winner of weekly sales contests with $25 awarded to the employee with the highest sale.

Overall, we strived for better working conditions and recognition and job security and these were surely a boost for morale in our organization.

Lessons Learned

- *Be concerned about the needs of your employees.*

- *Create good working conditions.*

- *Delegate responsibilities and make people feel needed and important.*

- *Motivate your employees and strive for good relationships.*

CHAPTER 15

Creating Good Customer Relations

Prelude

The backbone of a successful business is the ability to create revenue and profit. Of course, the providers of this most important ingredient are the customers who give patronage and loyalty. Your salespeople must constantly put forth all efforts to keep good customer relations.

Sales revenue is a direct result of customer satisfaction and patronage. All efforts mut be pointed at the bottom line -- the cash register.

The formula for shopper support is a composite of merchandising, quality, value and service. This concentration will bring buyers to your business and encourage repeat sales which will create more revenue and profit.

Merchandising is the selection and fashion of the inventory as presented to your specialized consumer and pointed to the type of market catered to for particular products.

The extent of quality is measured by the cost and the patron expectations.

In today's economic times, customers expect fair value for their dollars more so than in many recent years. Putting all the ingredients together to keep the purchasers happy and returning again must be topped off by good service. Not enough emphasis is placed on caring and consideration by businesses, but clients remember the special attention given them by courteous sales clerks. This can give the competitive edge to make a difference. Strategize programs to build customer satisfaction, including suppliers where possible to participate.

Coralling good public relations is accomplished by a good front line -- your salespeople. These are the people who have the most contact with your prospects and represent the business on a direct basis to the customers. They are at the forefront who give the first and last impression, and must be ready, willing and be knowledgeable of the merchandise to keep their interest. Your salespeople are the ones who make the sales and entice the buyers to return to your store.

A strong concentrated effort must be made not only to retain all old clientele, but emphasis and marketing techniques must be innovated to build an entire new patron base. Search areas which would appeal to people who have not patronized you in the past. Whether it be new products, quality or special services -- you must be creative for new attractions. This, of course, will have a positive effect on the old as well as the new.

Listen closely to the needs of your customers and watch carefully as to their reaction to change. Strive to create the reputation of being incomparable in the marketplace.

Building more interest will make your customers more responsive and their patronage is what goes hand in hand toward your needs of progress. Everyone looks to sales and service as the criteria for good customer relationships. Put heavy access and concentrate on a very potent change to make it happen.

Be objective in creating a strong purchaser base by working to perfect their views and needs. Think as if you were the spenders and be responsive to his/her perceptions.

The most accurate indication and market analysis of how your business is doing is by customer reaction. Encourage your salespeople to interact with them and to bring back their opinions and comments. Find out their responses as to products and service and use this information to benefit and help for changes. Marketing techniques are basically built around your present and potential shoppers' needs.

Customer satisfaction is based on the business giving them the products, assistance, and values they expect to receive. You cannot deviate from any part of this package. Always think of what your buyers are looking for and supply them with their desires. Your interests are secondary.

Your market dictates the items you sell and your consumers' response based on their socioeconomic, environment, personal, and family status ensures their acceptance.

Never underestimate the importance of good employee attitudes, concerns, and interest for your public, who deserve your respect and attention. Many times this makes the difference between you and your competition.

Make a study of your customers. Spot check them and discuss their thoughts to get further input. If certain products are not selling, get some frank opinions why. Watch their habits and choices and listen to their comments.

Play into your peoples' likes and eliminate their dislikes. Determine their preference of payment -- whether cash, check, or credit; then adapt your procedures accordingly. Make as many changes as necessary to improve their acceptance of your business.

A business is always built around the clientele. They have full discretion to spend their money anywhere they choose -- so the burden is on you to make it worthwhile for them to give you their allegiance. They have a right to expect fair values for their money, good service, pleasant and knowledgeable salespeople, and overall satisfaction.

The axiom that "the customer is always right" is a true statement that cannot be disputed because "that's where the buck stops." Your market study must be geared toward the purchasing power, the accpetable products, and the needs of those who patronize your business.

Customer revolution is as important to your turnaround goals as your operation, creditors and all others who are affecting your business.

Strategies that Worked in My Business

Our sales clerks were consistently reminded that the "Kings" and "Queens" of our business were the customers.

They were the ones who directed all our activities and all our actions. The merchandise we bought, how they were displayed, and the people who presented them always kept our patrons in mind.

In the midst of all our stores, we were up against competition with larger firms, more advertising dollars and sometimes a bigger variety of merchandise. Our distinction was the service, product knowledge and attention we gave our customers. We were intent on understanding their needs for the commodities they desired. Price didn't always make the difference. The care and interest did.

The buyers who visited our stores felt the hospitality and warmth as soon as they entered with friendly greetings. They immediately received the feeling that we were there to help with product assistance, their selections, or just to answer any questions. Our reputation in this area was well received.

Many times our efforts and courtesies weren't forgotten, and numerous phone calls and letters were sent to our office complimenting our sales clerks. On the other hand, we acted expeditiously on any complaints, which through the years were minimal.

I truly believe that our attitudes and interest to our "Kings" and "Queens" were the keynotes to our many years in business.

Lessons Learned

- *Customer satisfaction is key to business success.*
- *Concentrate on quality, value and service.*
- *Repeat sales builds volume and profit.*
- *Pay close attention and concentrate on needs of customers.*

CHAPTER 16

Gain The Confidence Of The Outside World

Prelude

> *Gaining the support and confidence from your creditors is a necessity to regain your business status. Past history of performance and your plans for improved management will play an integral part in your road to survival.*

An integral key behind everything is a good relationship with your creditors. They could drastically hurt you, or be a great asset to your comeback. If through the years you have been a loyal and profitable account, the "points" you have earned and the credibility and reputation you have gained will go a long way toward their working with you in troubled days. Most will want to help you get back on your feet and go forward again. Your approach and sincerity is important to keep their confidence.

Creditors and loaning institutions want to feel somewhat comfortable that despite declining sales, unproportionate overhead and increased operational expense that review of sound management tactics and a thorough evaluation of the company will help change its direction for a stable and upward trend.

You have to realize the position that the people you owe money to are in to share your problems -- because they have a stake in your destiny; therefore, to maintain and gain their confidence is worth the effort because they are the backbone to your survival.

Sharing your problems and levelling with them; discussing solutions and steps you are taking, will help to gain your creditors' confidence and support. Work up a realistic plan with your office staff or accounting firm based on projected sales and expenses for paying your indebtedness back. Sharing good intent on your goals -- even over a long designated term in conjunction with monthly or periodic payments will certainly demonstrate good faith efforts. This surely will make your creditors more comfortable and patient with your cash flow problems.

Earning credibility goes a lot further than just dealing with creditors. The total formula for a successful business comprises many ingredients, which must be combined to mold a finished product or profitable operation.

The most important part of the entire principle for success are the customers. Without the people who choose to patronize your business, nothing else will matter. The "buck stops there" if spending dollars for your merchandise and or services does not happen. Treat them as if they are the important part they play. They expect and deserve courtesy, service, and value -- and in return you will gain their patronage and confidence.

A motivated, loyal, and conscientious staff and work force must be built and maintained to keep the organization thriving. Ironically enough, salary or compensation is not all that is significant to earn the employees' reliability and respect. They expect a little more to feel like an integral part of the team. Company benefits, working conditions, and sensitivity of being needed increases morale and trustworthiness from the people who are your biggest day to day contacts for the business.

Landlords who you must deal with to make you comfortable and functionable in your facilities must be satisfied because the original lease and arrangements sometimes have to be adjusted and the property owner's cooperation must be gotten. They surely want their tenants to be successful so as to protect their investments.

Following rules, regulations and laws from your local, state and federal authorities further gives you the fine reputation to operate a company.

Some business relationships are warm and in many cases close social friendships prevail. Whether it be with customers, suppliers, or bankers, friends are helpful and appreciated in times of need. Your reputation and credibility is an asset you have built throughout the years and most people respect and recognize you as an honest and esteemed individual and generally do not forget.

The biggest attribute you must show is that same characteristic of your past in maintaining open phone lines and communication. Don't hesitate when requested to discuss cash flow problems and above all, never make an unrealistic commitment. People lose confidence quickly on false promises and your key players who you would look to for cooperation and help will dissipate. Excuses and delays will work once or twice, but then you will find yourself on "the list".

Your accountant and attorney are friendly consultants who are on your team and you should seek their advice and expertise on a regular basis or more frequently when necessary. A short chat with either at the right time could give you the impetus and direction to carry on.

Many times during my long years in business, I called my professionals to analyze and expound on issues, proposals and problems which were crucial and demanding. It is always helpful to get a listening ear and guidance to detect early warnings of problems during trying times.

I was a member of a buying association, and it was surprising how much peace of mind and information I received from my colleagues in networking on merchandising and systems. Our inter-exchange of ideas was a big asset for growth and existence.

Everyone you have contact with could be part of a support group to assist in adjustments.

It is easier to earn all your contacts' credibility because getting into the good habit of treating people right will "snowball" into everyone joining your bandwagon.

Leon Albin

Strategies that Worked in My Business

After going through the ordeal of slow pay and diminishing confidence by my suppliers, I worked up a plan to win back the faith of working together.

Our buying public never knew we were hurting, because we always kept our stores well stocked, current merchandise competitively priced and managed properly. However, our creditors and bankers knew of our struggling position. Those were the ones we had to convince of our comeback and regain their backing.

We put together a letter together with a proposed forecast and budget outlining our plans for the next six months and year, clearly describing our tightening up of operational costs and slower stores we intended to close. We showed anticipated profit and dollars available for cash flow and paybacks. We kept them abreast and goodwill phone calls were constant by me. They appreciated our communication and felt more assured and responsive.

Our employees were encouraged with straightforward talk as to what we all had to do together. They have seen the slower times, so levelling with them of our everyday agenda was appreciated. Generally, they went overboard to help find solutions. We took them into our confidence; they responded with their extra efforts. Our management people spent more time at the working level, and this gave the general employee more impetus to produce more effectively.

Our realization and acceptance of the facts and sharing this information with all those involved helped us in keeping everyone more comfortable and in the fold.

Lessons Learned

- *You must be aware of how your actions will impact the perceptions of your creditors.*
- *Work to keep them "comfortable".*
- *Share your turnaround plans.*
- *Make them feel like stakeholders in your future.*

- *Set interim realistic measurable targets and show creditors how you are meeting them to build credibility.*

- *Focus on your other constituents: landlords, customers, state and federal authorities, suppliers, bankers, buying associations.*

CHAPTER 17

Negotiating Under Pressure

Prelude

When the heat gets hot, don't lsoe your ability and composure to negotiate proper needs. Understanding your business requirements together with a keen proposal to negotiate a deal will make you stronger and more confident to reach the appropriate decisions.

The art of negotiating in business is a most important attribute under normal circumstances; but to be forced into this situation under trying times becomes somewhat awkward and puts one in a disadvantaged position to fulfill a deal at a fair price or terms.

When monies are tight and the heat is hot, and the vendors are harassing you for payments, keep cool with a clear head. Don't allow them to put you in a position or make commitments you can't keep.

Work on your strengths -- the many profitable years and the faith and ability to bounce back. Impress your creditors with good intentions and discuss doable arrangements with which you feel comfortable. Precedence of disbursements must be given to payroll, utilities, insurance protection and rents. Then you should divide and spread your payments to your creditors, keeping in mind that your key suppliers who are necessary for your continuance must be first in line.

Use your negotiating skills to push your main suppliers to work with you and support your good intent. Get as much cooperation as possible. Sell them on your confidence and work to get theirs.

Arbitrating involves several factors to successfully accomplish your goal or purpose.

Firstly and most importantly, you must understand the market, supply and demand. These conditions dictate the fair and lowest consideration which will ultimately be accepted. When the market and supply are flooded or heavy and the demand is light, the purchaser has the biggest bargaining power; and conversely if the market and supply is light and the demand is heavy -- then the seller or supplier has the edge.

Stamina and holding power allows a potential purchaser or user to put himself in a position to stall long enough to gain toward making his best deal. Pressure to hurry up the negotiations can wave the flag of desperation and "give your hand away".

Understanding the product or deal is necessary in your mediations -- as it will also tend to lessen any pressures. Knowing what you are talking about will keep you as the driving force in the discussions, as well as at what point you will be willing to increase your offer.

A meeting of the minds gives you the opportunity to loosen the burden and fixed indebtedness which are strangling the business. All areas affecting your ability to continue must be studied and a plan worked to confer these resources such as creditors, loans, leases, etc.

This could preclude trouble before it starts.

Concurring is a big part of the business agenda. Discussions and talks on financial needs, purchasing, terms, employees and customers are all part of the art of negotiating. Subject matters could cover anything with anyone affected and interested in your company, and happens constantly from day to day. It is very important and deserves deep concentration and skills.

Dealing with people in person goes further than on the phone; however, don't hesitate to work through the phone if necessary.

Train yourself to be prepared to the extent you are setting your sights on in order to achieve your goals. Be sure you are clear in your mind as to what you are trying to accomplish. Be ready to accept less because a good negotiator must be willing to compromise to make a deal. Think of all views and interests; don't only be concerned about your needs, but your plan must also understand the other side. Make allowances, when necessary, to produce your gains. After you have won your points, don't overkill.

Thinking back over the years, I can recall four incidents where attempts to agree commanded strong fortitude and staying control. I had to determine what I was driving for -- how low to start my offering and how high I could go to reach the limit.

The first occurrence of mediating which comes to mind involved my same store two doors from my competitor as mentioned in a previous chapter. It so happened that when my lease expired, my landlord wanted to double my rent. More importantly, was that in order to upgrade our image, it was imperative that I move in the area to a "fresh" location. I found the perfect site two blocks away on the same street, twice the size as the other and much more suited for our new merchandising trend.

Now started the deliberations to buy the building. In the beginning it appeared very simple. It was on the market for

$40,000 and very much affordable. I called the sales representative and told them I was prepared to buy the building. Two days later I got a call that the owners now want $50,000. I stalled for a few more days and then let them know that I would accept the increase. Instead of receiving a contract, another phone conversation informed me that the heirs were dickering and the price changed to $60,000.

At this point I became very annoyed and gave thought whether or not to drop it. This is where my restraint played a big part. I knew I needed a store in that market; there were no other places available; and even though the original price would have been a steal -- there was room in my budget. I pulled myself together and informed the sellers that I would accept. It didn't take long before the price became $70,000. Of course, there were "reasons" why and again I thought long and hard whether to pull out of the whole situation. Again, I let them know that I would complete the purchase. Well, once more they were bold enough to come back with a few more excuses and apologies that the figure was now $80,000. My response to this was obviously I have an interest in purchasing the building, but that you more than hit the limit, and either send me a contract for $80,000 to sign -- or forget it.

I finally paid $80,000 -- twice as much as the original offering -- but well within what our business could bear. Actually, this location became one of our most profitable shops -- and opened up the doors for several future stores, as it gave us direction and the impetus for our change of merchandising. Even though this negotiation experience was on the upward side -- rather than lowering the price or reaching a happy medium -- nevertheless, it proved that the important thing was to exert control and restraint to obtain my objective rather than abandoning the area after fifteen years.

Another trial and tribulation I was faced with was years later when I again stepped up our merchandising and types of locations. I felt our chain was ready to look to malls, rather than neighborhoods and strip centers. Little did I realize that most shopping centers leased a given space and a shell of a building, but expected the tenant to complete the internal portion of a finished structure. This, of course, would be a tremendous burden and could squelch any thought of getting into the mall.

After long deliberation and careful evaluation, I decided, unlike the previous experience, that I would convince the developers that we were needed to round out their tenant mix. I was prepared to "play hard ball" and look for a good deal or drop the idea.

I sold them on our elaborate plans in fixturing and the products we carry, which would blend into the traffic they needed and the investment necessary to open our doors. It took a few months, but following the process of going back and forth regarding our rent and construction costs, I was fully determined to put the "ball in their court". We finalized signing a lease with extremely low rent and their paying the full $75,000 required to build the entire store after they constructed the shell. In fact, when I ultimately sold my chain the low rental in this location was a big factor in our selling price. The adamant perseverance had paid off.

Throughout my years in business, knowing my merchandise, being completely familiar with the market, understanding my suppliers and being aware of my competitors' techniques were all important and significant factors in negotiating for every facet of operating my venture.

Practical Points to Negotiate

- Come prepared
- Utilize your strengths
- Know and understand your position
- Keep in back of your mind what you are striving for
- Consider the other side's arguments as important
- Respect their interests and convince them of yours

- Be fair and understanding in your debating and discussions

- Mediation is variable, so don't hesitate to expect to give and take

- Size up the bottom line of the other side

- Make everyone comfortable in your negotiations

- Be prepared to give in on an alternate option

- Use your influence and respect

- Use a pleasing personality

- Be convincing

- Start with bigger expectations so as to leave room to compromise

- Don't hesitate to bring another associate in to complete the negotiations, so as to soften the other side's position.

Dealing with bankers also takes deep fortitude, mediation, bargaining and shopping around. Negotiating usually takes strain and must be evaluated and studied for right decisions.

Strategies that Worked in My Business

Most suppliers were understanding and cooperative with us, but too many were tough and made us "sweat" to make a good deal.

I recall very vividly the extreme stress I was subjected to during my payout schedule when things were rough. Arranging for purchases were very trying when monies were due. In addition to the normal chores necessary to operate a sound business, I found myself with a new burden of appeasing my suppliers for shipments of other merchandise.

Even though I was working under constraints, I was able to show no tense emotions. My normal responses to "no shipments at this time" was "let's work out a percentage of payment to a ratio of new merchandise." Despite partial compensation, it showed good faith on my part. Generally, the new merchandise was much larger than the amount due. I was able to continue this arrangement because I proved, as time went on, that I lived up to my promises.

Knowledge of my products, keeping my needs at minimum quantities, and understanding my creditors' positions gave me the strength to accomplish my negotiations. Confidence and past history played a big part in convincing my suppliers that our company was a good risk.

Lessons Learned

- *Be sensitive to what's happening in the outside world.*
- *Be patient; don't give your hand away.*
- *Define the points you can be flexible on and then you will know when to compromise.*
- *Exercise restraint; be prepared to walk away, realizing the strength of your position.*

CHAPTER 18

Evaluate Your Lease

Prelude

Rent is a major expense in your operation. Therefore, the re-evaluation of your lease has to be dealt with as a serious item. Consideration must be given to the option of renewal or moving to meet the needs of a changing market.

Your rent could be a big backbreaker and needs some serious attention. Through the term of your lease, profits could have been good and this payment was not a concern -- as no doubt it was thought of as a normal and untouchable expense. However, economic and other conditions change and affect your location.

Firstly, your market could become different with population trends and a new transition character. Secondly, added competition could be taking a slice of the pie and hurting your business. Another factor could be additional shopping centers that attract people and pull customers from your area. Other stores vacating their premises means loss of traffic in your vicinity.

When any of the above happens, it is time for you to take a hard look to make an attempt to do something about your agreement.

Tighting up some loose ends on your lease or gaining an edge from your landlord still might not be enough for you to survive due to the conditions as mentioned above. If you come to realize that your present location is just a poor site and is not generating enough traffic flow, the proper step very likely would be to make attempts to terminate the contract and move to a stronger location.

Leases are binding and must be dealt with in a serious manner. These are usually the largest of your fixed expenses. There are times when the lessee is in a good position to reduce some of these charges. Supply and demand in that area may have a strong impact on re-negotiating an agreement. If the area is deteriorating, or heavier competition of openings, the landlord does not want to risk more vacant space. He or she might feel obliged to listen to a request for a reduction.

In considering the above, figure the termination of the current lease, moving expenditure and new set-up costs as well as higher rent in the new location. A projection of the potential higher sales must be budgeted to make your decision if the move is workable and practical.

Since rent consumes a large percentage of the operational disbursements, a strong look at possibly changing its economic terms plays a big factor in cutting back.

If you have come to the conclusion that your location needs to be moved -- for whatever reason -- you have this option if your lease has expired. Otherwise have an attorney review if there is any out clause or legal basis for lapsing. The right location is of top importance in your continuing on a profitable basis.

Consideration should be given to relocating at a more affordable rental; attempt to change the agreement with your present landlord; tighten up, give up some space, or sublet. Try to get a sympathetic ear from the owner to listen to your dilemma.

On the other hand, if you like your location, try negotiating with the landlord and appeal to him that you have economic basis, a market change or competition. Be prepared to show your backup information of statements reflecting your request of lower rents. If you have been a solid tenant you might have a chance.

C.P.I. (Consumer Price Index) is part of many lease agreements. This provision could be tagged on to the rent every year; only on option to renew; or at any period designated and agreed. This protects the owners from inflation and gives them the benefit of increases based on the higher dollars in future years.

Check your lease if you have the right to sub-divide or reassign. Your fixed obligations on rental fees could be a major factor in your battle for survival. The expression "working for the landlord" is a factual statement which is so often true. After evaluating that your rent percentage to sales is higher than the average in your industry, or is a figure you cannot justify, you should attempt to act to adjust this problem.

Strategies that Worked in My Business

Since rent is the biggest fixed expense and I was determined to lower costs, I had a lot of thinking to do about how to modify this overhead. I had seventeen leases to study to see if there were any loopholes or even changes in the areas or conditions that would avail me the opportunity to review and appeal to landlords or their management representatives to alter.

Owners of properties are concerned about new malls and how increased competition would affect traffic, sales and potential in their developments. Jeopardizing successful continuance diminishes acceptance and value of their property. Also, businesses or attractions that vacate have tremendous influence on the remaining stores. These are points and arguments I made in instances to adjust rents or consider abandoning when I had the opportunity.

By examining our agreements, I was able in one location to enforce a clause that if two thirds of the mall was not occupied within one year, I would have the discretion to convert from a fixed rent to a percentage of sales. This, of course, was a great savings and changed a losing store to one which became profitable.

We had a store which was dropping in sales with one year remaining. We were locked in, but after studying the lease, I found a weak occupancy and use clause and was able to change to an outlet store. This allowed us to dump all of our obsolete and slow moving merchandise from our entire chain. It accomplished two things -- unloading inventory and generating volume. At the end of the term, we vacated, but had used that location to a good advantage.

There was a new mall opening near one of our sites, and we were able to make a settlement with the owners of our place, and then moved to the newer and larger shopping center with major stores.

In another lease, we exercised our assignment rights to another tenant for two years, taking a loss, but we gained by eliminating other operational costs. We also experienced savings in two other stores by consolidating into smaller space with landlords' consents.

In another instance, we used some pressure when a lease with an option for renewal with increased rent expired. By being on top of our rights and threatening to terminate, we were able to continue without any additional requirements.

Leon Albin

I found out studying leases gave us unexpected opportunities and made me smarter for future agreements.

Lessons Learned

- *Don't feel tied to current locations because of leases.*
- *Evaluate the economics of rent paid against cost of breaking your lease and changing locations.*
- *Look at the overall economic impact to your business.*
- *Decide if you are in the right location, and then act accordingly.*

Lease Amendment Form

Landlord and _____, Tenant,

under a lease agreement between them for property

_____, hereby amend said Lease as follows:

This lease amendment shall be binding upon and all

parties, their successors, assigns, associates and executors.

All other lease terms shall remain as written in the original

Lease.

_____ _____ _____ _____(SEAL)
Witness   Date   Landlord   Date

_____ _____ _____ _____(SEAL)
Witness   Date   Landlord   Date

Sublease Agreement Form

1.   This sublease was entered into between

_____ (Tenant) and

_____ (Subtenant).

2.   The Subtenant agrees to lease _____

_____ (property location)

from _____ to _____

3.   The Subtenant agrees with all terms and conditions of the lease entered into by the Tenant. The Subtenant agrees to pay the Landlord the monthly rent and any additional expenses provided.

4.   The Subtenant agrees to pay to Tenant the sum of $_____ as a security deposit.

5.   The Subtenant agrees to pay the Tenant the sum of $_____ in consideration of this agreement.

6.   Attached to this agreement is a list of equipment and fixtures that were in the above property at time of sublease. The Subtenant agrees to replace or reimburse the Tenant for any of these items that are missing or damaged and to repair the premises to its original condition.

7.   The Landlord consents to this sublease and agrees to promptly notify the Tenant at _____

_____ if the Subtenant is in breach of this sublease agreement. Tenant shall remain obligated under this lease.

_____ _____ _____ _____(SEAL)
Witness   Date   Tenant   Date

_____ _____ _____ _____(SEAL)
Witness   Date   Subtenant   Date

_____ _____ _____ _____(SEAL)
Witness   Date   Landlord   Date

CHAPTER 19

Restructure Financing

Prelude

Recreating financial support is necessary to continue and maintain your business existence. The relationship with your banker or association with a new bank is urgent to restructure financing as a strong tool to eliminate possible bankruptcy.

The financial backbone of a business is the life blood for survival. Despite a lack of surplus funds, there still must be a cash flow in order to operate on a day-to-day basis. Before looking to outside financial help, be sure your own remedy has been exhausted.

This is one area that the accounting firm representing you could play a significant part. Their expertise in preparing current statements, and comparing and evaluating previous years' information is the key to a presentation which could be acceptable to a financial institution for refinancing or maintaining your current credit line. Your lender will want to see updated as well as comparative information, cash analysis, balance sheets and profit and loss statements.

Your banker is your target to strengthen your financial chaos by restructuring your loan arrangement. The undertaking to convince your bank to revise your debts must include your accountant and lawyer so that your presentation is done professionally and effectively.

You must learn to understand the type of person your banker is -- and allow him or her to know you and your business to build a more compatible and workable rapport.

It is always good, sound business sense to keep in touch with your banker. Invite him to your office periodically as they always feel better seeing firsthand what is happening to their money.

Being thorough and candid with your banker will build a relationship with confidence and trust, which will prevail

Leon Albin

upon them the flexibility to extend themselves in times of need.

Prepare your presentation to your banker with adequate information which should include at least three years of financial statements, and business and personal tax returns.

Give a convincing and clear picture as to your business operation; where it fits into the marketplace; why the loan is needed; and how it will be repaid.

Plan your credit line long before you have the need. Your approval is diminished if you try to arrange a loan application on short notice.

Decisions on loans are generally made based on company liquidity, so your banker will examine your percentage of assets to liabilities to determine your strength. The ratio can vary from two to one, or even three to one or higher, and is based on the type of business, competition, and stability.

It is a banker's business to make loans -- but as good business people, banks are cautious in their transactions.

Their loans result in interest, which creates profit. However, just as a business must build sales to make a profit, so do loaning institutions find it incumbent on their operation to mold deposits to have ability to make loans and prosper.

Loans must follow certain strict patterns for banks to be successful. Therefore, for the businessperson to expect and obtain loans, he or she must be convincing to the banker for consideration.

You, as the applicant, must firstly have the banker know your character as one who can be trusted. Secondly, you must show your ability to repay on the terms agreed. In some cases the bank might issue a credit line by just a signature -- but this is rare. Generally the borrower must have adequate collateral to protect the loaner if the repayment plan is not met.

Cooperate with your banker, give him or her proper information to extend the loan, and let the banker understand your business and how the funds will be used. Create a good impression to have them feel relaxed with you, and be a friend on your side.

A key responsibility in accepting the bank's money from a loan is to supply them with timely statements. Banks are required by federal regulations to maintain records of each loan.

The financial institution realizes that without steady, frequent statements there is a likely problem and might be alerted as to a downward business trend. You cannot ignore the importance of making your banker comfortable.

Adequate time must be taken by you and your professionals who evaluate all the data to find the pertinent and salient points, so as to be convincing to these banks or financial groups. In addition to being carefully scrutinized, you could be subjected to a higher interest. Further, depending on net worth of your company, you very likely might be required and expected to sign a personal guarantee.

Realistically, if the company's net worth is weak or negative, your chances for a strong financial restructuring will be very difficult. Obviously, your strongest chances for the bank's support is to catch your problems early. Therefore, the best opportunity for expanded financial support is to study your business trends on a regular basis in order to detect possible needs of help.

Try to steer clear of your loaner while fighting the cash flow and creditor problems. Don't alert or spark their attention. If they call on you for a reevaluation, contact your accountant to give you the best financial statement possible, taking into consideration future budget based on improved cash flow.

Your relationship with your banker and his/her confidence in you and your company is fully the basis of the decision on how to react to your approach when you have a problem.

Your lending institution could either recall the loan in full -- or can refinance the debt so that the principal is extended over a longer period, and thus lower your monthly pay-out.

As soon as you are notified by your bank for a review, contact a back-up source to prepare for a possible change. Be positive and optimistic and study if a new bank would have additional benefits of affordable interest rates and flexibility for small businesses.

There are several areas to investigate and look for financing or restructuring of monies for your business. Not one is simple or easy, and each source might be tougher than the other to convince them of the secure and low risk to move forward with you. The better position you are in -- the financial statements, presentation, forecasting and budgeting -- dictates the availability, interest and consideration.

1. The easiest method to obtain money is your own savings -- selling stocks, etc.

2. The next means is through friends or family -- but beware of the risk of personal relationships.

3. The conventional first place to go in your bank. After their evaluation and possibly unrealistic collateral, high limits, ratios and interest to work with, you no doubt would be inclined to shop elsewhere.

4. You may try government assistance of either federal or state programs for the small business person. They may work with guarantees in conjunction with your private lenders. If you qualify, you might be eligible with a high percentage guaranteed government loan.

5. There are organizations that specialize in small business loans. It would be worthwhile to investigate if any are available in your area for your type of business and for your kind of needs.

6. Some venture capitalists will invest in a company in exchange for equity if they feel their risks are limited -- or

greater, if the shares of equity are substantial in relation to their investments.

7. Another method of raising funds is obtaining a second mortgage. Of course, you must have adequate equity remaining in the property since the priority of any default would go to the first mortgagee. Also the interest rate would be at a premium and much higher than the original loan since the risk is much greater.

8. Other areas to help debt rearrangement are outside lending institutions, investors, creditor cooperation, or asset reduction.

Always be cognizant of balloon loans which can become part of your borrowing arrangement. These types of loans are written to cover a certain number of years with principal and interest the same every month over that period. However, the "balloon" kicks in at an agreed time of the loan (usually halfway) and then the entire balance is either recalled or negotiated for a new higher interest rate. This protects the bank or loaner against inflation or any possible loss.

Most people do not understand this terminology and are in the dark as to its meaning. Be sure your attorney reviews and explains this condition of your loan.

Restructuring financing is a strong step in eliminating possible bankruptcy. Both bankers and creditors alike would be cooperative in helping to deter a failure since their interest is to salvage monies due against potential losses.

Strategies that Worked in My Business

Just as I had to constantly convince creditors of my good faith to keep their confidence and trust, so too did I take very seriously the role of my financial backers. I understood and respected their characteristics of being conservative and structured and dealt with them accordingly.

I was always able to finance my business with our company funds, creditors and bankers. I never found it necessary for other money people who were known for high interest rates. In rearrangement for any loans, my thoughts were not to consider any other sources, but to continue to maintain the sound confidence of my present people. My position was to hold things the way they were and not to "rock the boat."

My accountant and I were in close touch with my banking officer, and supplied him with accurate information to retain his comfort. Then, at the appropriate time, I set up a meeting to extend the notes due with longer spreads of payments. This loosened up our pressures with them, and allowed me to fit their obligations in on a timely and prompt basis.

I also found it very helpful with the mass quantities of inventory we held, and rather than look for more funds to meet obligations, we would once a year set up a warehouse sale to unload certain replaceable or excess stocks. This provided us with additional resources, instead of getting in deeper with lending institutions.

Lessons Learned

- *Get to know your banker.*

- *Build a strong relationship.*

- *Provide full information on where funds are to be employed.*

- *Show liquidity.*

- *Consider all options to arranging financing.*

CHAPTER 20

Bankruptcy As a Strategic Option For Survival

Prelude

> *When all efforts have failed and the creditors' pressures become*
> *unbearable, unrealistic and impossible to cope with, a chapter 11*
> *or 13 Bankruptcy can be a savior for an undetermined period.*
> *This could give you an opportunity to reorganize your failing*
> *business back to a viable condition.*

Most people think of bankruptcy as the ultimate end -- full liquidation. There are two types of bankruptcies, however, which businesses or individuals can enter into within the courts for protection and reorganization. Chapter 11 can be adaptable for any debts for corporations, partnerships or individuals. Chapter 13 can be used for individuals only with unsecured debts not exceeding $250,000 and secured debts not exceeding $750,000. Both should be avoided if possible and entered into only as a final option for survival.

Even though statistics show that only approximately twelve percent of those that enter Chapter 11 or 13 ever work their way out, it is still a viable direction to pursue if other alternatives for a turnaround solution seem to be failing. Given this reorganization opportunity could be the last ditch option to save the business. This book discusses direction for the "step before bankruptcy", but Chapter 11 or 13 Bankruptcy can be the savior needed to survive. This form of bankruptcy is available to businesses and individuals if they can produce a viable method of reorganization which would be validated by the courts.

Despite your intense and exerted turnaround efforts, your business survival might only be possible and realistic if helped by a Chapter 11 or 13 Bankruptcy condition. You probably will be cut back and the "cat skinned", but it is not always a sound direction to work on saving the entire business. In many instances, survival should be directed at consolidation.

It makes good business sense to get out of the operation and salvage the viable parts.

Remember the road to recovery is a long, tedious process -- but your creditors, bankers and employees are anxious for you to prevail because they all have something to benefit. Even though your creditors will sustain considerable losses, they will gain a larger percentage of their debts as well as the opportunity of continued sales and profits if you remain in business. Bankers also would be paid a larger portion of their loans -- and very likely will be paid in full -- especially if they were personally secured. Employees will be happy and have a higher incentive and morale to keep their jobs.

Our laws allow a business or individual under Chapter 11 or 13 to put holds for repayment with the burden and responsibility on the debtor with creditors' approval to present a reorganization and repayment plan. This procedure in most cases will allow an agreed period of time to pay the debts and at a percentage of total invoices. The overall scheme must be satisfactory to those due monies that the plan indicate a turnaround and the ability to continue. They must convince all that the management team will be effective to change the operation; that sales can be increased while expenses can be reduced; that it is in the best interest of the creditors; and that the business or individual is acting in good trust.

The temporary relief under a Chapter 11 or 13 reorganization plan is that upon filing, the debtor receives immediate relief from all creditors and bankers of paying debts except those that are nondischargeable. These include fraud or embezzlement, alimony and child support, most taxes including withholding and social security. Also excluded are certain educational loans and fines for drunken driving. It is further the debtor's responsibility to file a petition with the courts within 120 days of declaring Chapter 11 or 13. After this period the debtor would be under the discretion of the court as to the status for a successful endeavor to operate the reorganization plan and be dismissed or to file for a full liquidation.

Although Chapter 11 is not a glamorous step to take in business -- nevertheless, it could be the saviour in times of distress. The temporary relief from creditors and bankers it provides gives you some "breathing room" to keep them at "arm's length".

This court protection gives you an extended period to recoup, replan, and rebuild with the opportunity of getting back on the right track. It takes real determination, toughness, and commitment to pull out of the Chapter 11 Bankruptcy Plan, but it can be do-able.

It has become more frequent for both small businesses and the giant corporate world to strategize around a bankruptcy plan to regain financial strength and sustenance, and even to move the company forward. The results have become better -- because both the creditors and financial institutions have come to realize that it is to everybody's advantage to cooperate to keep the business whole in order to protect their own investments for larger payments.

The primary purpose in filing for bankruptcy is to protect the business and/or the owners -- whether the filing is for reorganization or liquidation. You must seek professional assistance if you have any thought of a bankruptcy proceeding. An attorney specializing in this field will give you the appropriate advice and guidance as to your own preparation and how to deal with creditors and banks.

Your attorney and your accountant will weigh your options and put together a program which will best benefit your needs. In a voluntary bankruptcy there are many debts that could completely be relieved; others that can be settled and negotiated at a fraction of the debts; and others which will have programs for long pay-outs. A good reorganization plan can be a boost to a faltering business. In order for the court to approve the plan, the debtor must prove the capability to meet the pay-back plan and that the creditors are satisfied and comfortable. The debtor has 120 days to satsify the court with an acceptable plan.

Filing for a voluntary bankruptcy can bring new life into your organization if your plan protected and agreed by the courts adequately covers your capability to bounce back and get on your feet. The stay and relief from your creditors together with hard action in tightening up your overhead can immediately give you the opportunity of regaining your composure to reorganize.

If your situation has gone too far in the red and you will not be able to satisfy a court reorganization plan, your bankruptcy can turn to a liquidation of all your assets. At that time creditors, through a forced sale, will derive a fraction of their receivables from your company. It is therefore to everybody's advantage to see a Chapter 11 or 13 work -- so that the payback can be as much as possible.

A Chapter 7 involuntary bankruptcy will mean full liquidation -- fraction paybacks. In distribution of assets, the secured creditors have the highest priority -- those that are collateralized or have personal guarantees.

An involuntary bankruptcy is brought about by three or more creditors with combined claims of $5,000 or more who protest to the bankruptcy court that the debts are past due.

A business with financial problems should seek advice and counselling from a qualified attorney in the field of bankruptcy. By all means, this service must be retained immediately upon notification of a petition for an involuntary bankruptcy proceeding. There is protection that can be sought based on improper information. Your attorney can quickly develop tactics and techniques to possibly overcome this petition -- basically by proving to the court that his client is not in arrears in debts. Also, the creditors might be shown that it is to their advantage to change the involuntary to a voluntary bankruptcy with an agreeable plan.

In bankruptcy proceedings, there are two classifications of claims. Priority is given to demands which are guaranteed by some sort of collateral, which is usually tied in through the courts with a security agreement. Unsecured debts have no special status for paybacks.

A major concern in filing for a voluntary bankruptcy is the stigma it creates for your business and associates to view. It could open up a "can of worms" and further risks.

Before entertaining any thoughts of this type of action, you must thoroughly meet and evaluate your entire financial condition with your accountant and attorney. They must be on your decision making team and give you advice as to timeliness on whether to "hang in there" and exert your company's effort for your internal turnaround. Many times honest discussions with your creditors and bankers and an unofficial plan instead of bankruptcy will give the time you need.

The cost for your own work-out with professional consultants is thousands of dollars less than an act of bankruptcy. If you contact each creditor on a one-to-one basis and offer a percentage settlement like twenty-five to fifty percent to save your business -- letting them know that this is in lieu of further court protection, you probably will find this is acceptable and do-able to save your company.

The proceedings for bankruptcy is not a simple process and is very costly.

In today's economy, however, bankruptcy is a common practice and is used more today in our country than ever in our history. Your company's financial position could be insolvent or even solvent. Your balance sheets can be altered through the accounting process to appear in deeper financial straits to show insolvency; or on the other hand you can show a balance sheet with assets having more net value and a stronger asset to liability ratio.

Involuntary bankruptcy of chapter 11 or 13 can be a strong strategic option to maintain and continue the business, but it isn't always possible to bounce back from this program to gain strength and sustenance.

Bankruptcies aren't always triggered off by only liabilities, overpowering assets -- halting the lifeblood of the operation and creating a precarious position to continue. Bankruptcies also are ignited by traumatic situations that occur which will seriously and fatally affect the company. Occurrences which can set off this condition could be a tremendous and unexpected liability problem caused by lawsuits or damages and not covered by insurance. Uncontrollable labor troubles have caused bankruptcies, also.

Basically, bankruptcies happen in tough economic times -- but as mentioned, other factors bring about this court protection for the company. An internal decision could be made to have drastic changes in operation, personnel or leases. It could loosen areas which are tightly contracted, or a bankruptcy can give flexibility which could not be done in a conventional manner.

In the early part of the nineteenth century when bankruptcy laws started, it was very intimidating and unprotective. Even after liquidation, debtors found themselves bound to the responsibilities of repayment, and frequently found themselves in prison or physically harmed to satisfy the claims. Later in the middle 1800's, laws were changed to dismiss the debt.

The process has been simplified in the last twenty-five years; wherein, the court takes less involvement for reorganization plans and allows the debtors and creditors to work out negotiations and settlements.

Management under Chapter 11 can be the same organization -- but in many instances, changes of control gives the reorganization a new look, a new approach, and new decision making.

Reorganization is a preference over liquidation as everybody stands to benefit. If the creditors give the debtors an opportunity to work out a plan -- the step before bankruptcy -- they stand to reap more of a percentage on their receivables than a forced sale. This premise is, of course, if the business has adequate assets in relation to liabilities, despite a negative net worth.

Careful and thorough evaluations must be made to determine the company's tangible worth, taking into account the realistic assets and liabilities and considering immediate future changes. There are creditors who take precedence over others, depending on corporate or personal guarantees. Creditors in thier categorical position all get a proportionate share due them.

In a designed and planned reorganization, the company, along with professional help can work out a strategy and approach which can be acceptable and beneficial for all. Based on future projections, creditors and banks will receive a bigger return on monies due and in a more expedited manner.

Circumstances Which Cause Bankruptcy

- Incapable of leadership

- Slow decision making

- Management problems

- Irregular professional assistance

- Poor tax planning

- Financial information not maintained

- Not following financial direction

- Ineffective control of assets

- Sluggish forecasting and budgeting

- Inability to improve cash flow

- Lack of cost control

- Slow inventory turnover

- Unfamiliar with merchandise

- Poor merchandising

- Inadequate promotions

- Failure to keep up with market changes

- Inability to maintain pace with competitors

- Insufficient training programs

- Too much absenteeism

- Unsatisfactory supplier relationship

- Weak customer relations

- Ineffective employee relations

- Lack of follow up of receivables

- Under-insured

- Overextension of credit

- Too fast expansion

- Creditors clamping down.

As listed above, there are so many obstacles to overcome in order to consummate a reorganization. Unless you have a relentless determination to eliminate these drawbacks and disadvantages, which could cause your business demise, and show strong willpower and unyielding stamina, the chances are slim that you will be successful in this endeavor.

You must gain the confidence of your banker and creditors based on good faith, by convincing them of the merits of your plans and how it will benefit them for payment.

Be flexible in your approach to reorganization, taking into full account the effects of the economy, and the change of posture of everyone around you.   Try to make them feel comfortable that business is as usual.

In considering filing for Chapter 11 or 13, determine if you have enough time to turn the business around and if you feel you can reflect a reduction in expenses and stabilize or increase your sales. That is the basis for saving your business. You must feel that this option is worth pursuing for survival.

Another factor to consider is for you to recognize in yourself if you have the courage, fortitude, guts, the spirit and attitude to cope with the displeasure, tension, and aggravation.

Strategies that Worked in My Business

All the tension and stress that I was faced with from day to day would baffle my mind as to best alternatives and direction to take. I remained strong and convinced that I could come out of any situation that came up. It became a competitive challenge, and actually strengthened my tenacity and drive.

When I retained my bankruptcy attorney, my thoughts were to use our combined ingenuity in relentlessly holding the creditors back until I could make my turnaround. I was determined to program my own "unofficial" Chapter 11 to allow us the time necessary for the period needed to make my comeback.

Although I was aware of my limitations afforded a struggling business, and that it could be a reorganization savior for only an undetermined period, my plan was to do the same things available to satisfy creditors and bankers. In fact, I emphasized my intention, and reminded them that working with me will give them a much larger share of their receivables, even if we get to a settlement state.

I felt that it would take the same disposition and perseverance needed to do my own programming as it would with a Chapter 11 bankruptcy. The only difference is the protection from the courts against creditors of harassment and a possible forced Chapter 7 bankruptcy for total liquidation. I knew given time and patience I could work out of it myself without a stigma of bankruptcy.

My persistence succeeded, and the use of my "pay off" plan and settlements of those that were satisfied to accept up to one-third of my indebtedness, helped to resolve my negative position to where I was able to continue in business, or look for a buy-out.

Lessons Learned

- *There are two types of Bankruptcy proceedings: Voluntary is self-imposed; Involuntary is forced by creditors.*
- *Bankruptcy can be sudden and frightful.*

253

Leon Albin

- *Prepare for the unexpected by sound preparation from bankers' fears and suppliers' cut-offs.*

- *Develop a savior by a back-up plan of legal protection before it happens.*

.

CHAPTER 21

Take a Firm Hold on Rebuilding

Prelude

Having experienced tough times and having "nursed" your company back to a healthy state should put you in a position to think about rebuilding. Thinking positive for a brighter future and working a plan will make it possible to achieve realistic results.

The road to recovery is very trying and frustrating -- but it is made possible by your persistence and motivation to succeed. The information in this book makes the tedious task realistic and do-able but must be followed closely to reach the rebuilding process. Renewed interest and purpose must be realized and accepted by present management -- but it might be necessary to re-ignite the fuse with few new personnel.

After you have gotten somewhat comfortable in having conquered the many aspects of getting "back on track" to convince yourself that you can stay in business despite adversity, it's due time to move ahead.

The next move is to position yourself to rebuild -- because you have taken the steps backward in order to go forward, the preliminaries of lost confidence, getting people off your back, and restructuring. Change of direction to hold on must now shift to rebuilding and thinking ahead.

There is nothing more satisfying to an entrepreneur than knowing that the future looks brighter. This will never happen if you don't accomplish it. Think positive and set yourself toward a successful goal.

Just as you planned your survival and worked hard -- so must you now look to rebuild and look to a higher level than ever before. Set your standards to a realistic sight and work your plan to accomplish these goals. Map out your organizational structure so as to make it possible to achieve these realistic results.

Evaluate your past and based on flaws of "yesterday" reorganize your operation to reconstruct what can be done for "tomorrow". Putting things in place will be very challenging to motivate your future undertakings.

Don't hesitate to make changes of old methods to create the needs of today's standards. Rebuilding must take into account your past activities with a keen approach as to what is needed for your future operation.

You have been through all the steps on your comeback. Now you must put it all together to become aggressive in programs and systems. You certainly want to better your condition and move forward. All your goals must be realistic and you surely should intend to be careful not to go backwards, but discipline everyone to follow more controlled and regulated systems.

All the elements of the newly designed organizational program must be followed with minimal diversion. You must carefully review and scrutinize on a regular weekly basis each and every area which reflects the bottom line -- profits. Do not lose touch with incoming and outgoing monies -- as well as all those involved in making it happen.

Now that you have the right way, "tear apart" your office and thoroughly study its efficiency. Review all the routines of what the "heart" of your organization is doing and alter methodology immediately where new ideas would be more effective. Now is the time to rate each person as to his or her performance -- and if changes are in order, do it as soon as possible to improve.

Be prepared to modify procedures in your office and your system. All areas for rebuilding must be looked at and carefully studied and objectively evaluated for possible alterations and improvements in your organization.

The office operation was the first step -- but everything fails to move if you don't have enthusiastic and conscientious employees. They make it happen. Get them to be an integral part of the renewed process. Now more than ever you can't afford "dead wood" -- so watch your payroll carefully and make everyone accountable for their part in a sound recovery.

Help employee motivation and creativity.

Next, get the "pork" out of your advertising. Try to count results from your advertising dollars and cut down where management feels you can eliminate.

Marketing habits and areas covered might not be bringing you the returns necessary to enjoy a sound profit. Your spread of the marketplace might be too thin. A study must be done to evaluate where the income is highest and then the lower markets must be eliminated as the cost of doing business in these areas are probably hurting your bottom line.

Customers are your biggest asset. They are the ones that "ring the register". Treat each and everyone as if he or she is the most important person you are dealing with. They should always feel that their presence is welcomed; their business is most appreciated; and should be treated with respect and enjoy special service. A salesperson who is courteous and has product knowledge always comes across in a positive way. Training your clerks to carry good sales habits is beneficial to your business.

Finally, the rebuilding process revolves around the appropriate inventory which is timely, "fashionable", updated and related to the type of merchandise expected to be found in that type of store or warehouse.

Dead and obsolete inventory dilutes the look and acceptance of all the other merchandise -- so emphasis must be placed on the proper inventory. Proper displays and presentation is a big factor in customer acceptance.

During these trying times, watch carefully that there is no overload of inventory or dead merchandise as you surely can't afford to carry an extra load.

In looking to rebuild, you must search for new areas and opportunities to broaden your business. These can be expanding successful departments in your present operation, changing your methods, or even bringing in new ideas.

Search for new techniques and systems to increase your business.

- Introduce new merchandise in a related field which complements your image
- Broaden successful ideas for more depth and variety
- Cutback slower items
- Expand market ideas to other departments
- Eliminate lower priced merchandise where higher profits and acceptability can be obtained
- Trade up certain products that are more desirable
- Lower prices in certain categories and items for special leaders
- Transfer items to different departments to make them appear more desirable
- Package related items for higher sales
- Sell separately to push sales
- Cater to specialized customers.

The rebuilding process must be a dedicated and committed undertaking which requires heavy conscientious thought and activity. There are many steps for consideration to accomplish this feat:

- A new look
- Alter the mode of operation
- New physical facilities
- Different location
- Additional funding
- Need for higher sales volume
- Lowering of expenses
- More enthusiastic and inspired employees
- Stability of customers
- Position of competitors
- Economy outlook

A business can be put into a stronger and healthier condition, not only for survival, but for further progress if a beneficial merger with a similar operation can be effected. This direction can put new life in the current company as well as the added one, if the combined businesses can be compatible and work harmoniously together.

To avoid any future legal problems or misunderstandings, a merger or sale should be handled by an attorney. The agreement would address and spell out the assets and liabilities of both companies, officers and positions as well as duties and responsibilities. It would further clear up the financial obligations of both parties to their creditors.

The settlement would further detail payment terms, inventories and expenses due to close out and join with the other. It would also spell out effective date and valid signatures of officers.

The turnaround process could, if practiced and lived every day to its fullest, with complete concentration and thoughtfulness, be an exercise of habit and develop into a fruitful project. The re-structuring of the wheels and the operation of a company requires ingenuity and fortitude beyond imagination with a change of attitude and superb leadership.

Strategies that Worked in My Business

After coming as far as I did, there was no question as to what my next step would be. Now I set my sights for new growth and a rejuvenated outlook on my future and opportunities.

Saving a business doesn't necessarily suggest you must rebuild your organization for the purpose of continuing. It could indicate your interest in selling out or merging your company. The formality is the same; that is, prepare your business no matter which direction you choose: Tighten the right spots; update your systems; close losing stores;

consolidate and strengthen every unit. In other words, the preparation is exactly the same, whichever path you take.

I felt very confident that I had a worthy business -- not a distressful company -- and one deserving of holding my head up high. My past was behind me, and I was ready to move forward. I personally had meetings in each store with the manager and sales clerks to reignite the spark we always had.

Things that were necessary to do in order to get to a profitable position were being practiced by every store. We again reviewed our methods of doing business, ran a tight "ship," and were ready to go all out.

One day I received a phone call from the president of a national sporting goods chain. He wanted to enter our market we served, and asked me if I would be interested in a sell-out. After a few days of thought, I felt it was time, after 38 years, to consider. I called him back; then, he and his Chairman of the Board flew into Baltimore from Florida; spent one full day visiting my stores and its locations. Before they had left, they made me an offer "too good to refuse." We then met a week later in their office and a deal was made.

Rebuilding can result in continuance in business for yourself or making it desirable enough for a sell-out.

Lessons Learned

- *Be mentally, physically and financially prepared to move forward.*

- *Think positive and rebuild to future stability and success.*

- *Develop a sound organizational program with realistic goals.*

- *Never forget the importance of your employees and customers.*

- *Concentrate on strong marketing tactics.*

CHAPTER 22

Be Optimistic -- Yet Realistic

Prelude

After having overcome the many problems to stabilize your business, you must be more optimistic in looking ahead. Regain your confidence and respect and continue to rebuild your optimism.

Looking ahead to face the new problems after having stabilized your business is a new challenge which should give you a new lease on life. Once you have overcome the temporary set-back and keeping the creditors, financiers and suppliers at arm's length, you must build a sense of confidence to handle the necessary steps toward building a successful future.

Having gone through the horrifying experience of almost losing your business and hanging on thin ropes, being realistic as to choosing a strategy in the turn of your business will be helpful in mapping out a plan and making the right decisions.

Along with becoming more theoretical, you must feel proud as to what you have done in putting a shaky business back on track; and use this experience toward becoming optimistic in your mental outlook. Your mind now becomes a big factor in your future undertakings.

You no doubt built a successful business by doing the right things; and now you must utilize your past performance to be optimistic for the future. Obviously, you didn't last as long as you did if your ability wasn't there. Assure yourself that your "know how", your contacts, and above all, yourself, can now look at rebuilding with a real positive outlook to not only bring you back to the position before things went astray -- but feeling fully confident in yourself for doctoring up a sound business.

Being optimistic means believing in yourself. Be convinced of your ability. Enthusiasm is contagious and your demonstrating to the people around you that this fervor can rub off on them so as to support and work with you.

As the leader and the chief in your buisness, silent signals are spread all around you as to your own feelings. People get turned on or off as they watch and listen to you. All eyes and ears are around you -- and your indications and actions are symbolic as to theirs.

Evaluate your thoughts or ideas with your confidants and share some of your plans with those that have a working or pecuniary interest in your business. Showing that you are not wavering -- but have a strong will to accomplish with a very high opinion of yourself to go on to greater heights will bring people around you and will convince those needed that together you can do better. They will feel more comfortable and willing to cooperate with whatever it takes to go forward.

The old adage of following the leader is true and they will want to work with and emulate one who can show them the true spirit of believing in yourself. Corral people with honesty and integrity and they will believe in you and want you to succeed with their assistance wherever they can.

Together with a solid plan of action, reinforcing a good devoted team in your company, following a new "code of ethics" and regaining the confidence, respect and cooperation from your creditors and banker will continue to rebuild your optimism.

Strategies that Worked in My Business

During most of my years in business, I was fortunate in enjoying the good times, so when the trying periods came, I was able to remember the "good ole days," and stay optimistic as to what we could look forward to. We had overcome some heavy obstacles, so I had every reason to believe that the future looked bright.

At our monthly managers' meetings, we only spoke positive as to our goals, and each month we recognized and discussed what we had accomplished. We never forgot that things could be rough -- but constantly worked toward improving our situation. The employees became more encouraged as they saw day-to-day things happening again. Letdowns were few because they were part of all of us looking up. We were seeing the better side again, yet took on normal precautions.

Our suppliers again recognized us as a key account and seemed to work closer with renewed confidence. They were more involved with us; and became çautious to our advantage, so as to not recommend questionable items. This helped us to order prime merchandise that turned faster.

In one instance, there was a major athletic shoe line we purchased in large quantities and high volume. They suggested that we buy less -- the best items -- keep the inventory and bills low and help our cash flow.

Sales were not lost because the representative knew he would have to see us more frequently, so now our turnover

Leon Albin

became greater. He was optimistic but realistic not to see us get into the same predicament.

We had hope and faith in our strategy and were straightforward in our approach.

Lessons Learned

- *Be self-assured and positive.*
- *Be ready to work out future plans.*
- *Be realistic in your strategy.*
- *Be straight forward in your approach.*

CHAPTER 23

Profit From Your Mistakes

Prelude

Looking back and analyzing what went wrong will be very helpful in staying on the right track. Benefit by your past experiences and profit from your mistakes.

A temporary setback can even be helpful in the road to success. Evaluating carefully as to what brought you down and making a close study as to the problems it created can reveal the solution to make things happen in the right direction.

You cannot put the past aside and try to go on with the future, since every experience gives a lesson. What happened along the way and studying the major as well as minor errors will have a definite affect on curing these patterns for correction and perfection in rebuilding.

Every business should study its strengths and weaknesses and put exerted efforts toward the areas that should be boosted. Realizing the shortcomings is an important step to improvement.

A review and survey of your whole business and its past performance will help you profit for the future. A synopsis of things that happened "yesterday" will improve what will take place tomorrow. Study previous flaws and capitalize on costly errors.

You must look at operations, personnel, location, suppliers and virtually any facet of your business which affects the bottom line. Changing times and different merchandising must be reviewed and the fact that you might not have blended in with these new trends obviously could have been very significant factors toward business problems.

Looking at the past to create a new and better future is using this experience to a great advantage. There is no doubt that hind-sight would have had you do things differently -- so profitting by these oversights will be quite beneficial. Everything in life is an experience -- using this background is an integral part of changes and trends for the future.

Learning from your past faults will give you well-earned experience in your future endeavors. Utilizing these errors could make you a better business person if you study your previous habits. Be cognizant and ready to examine your former flaws, and be prepared to make changes within yourself, management, your employees and your operation. Rid your organization of your weaknesses, and play on your strengths.

Assess your methods of buying and selling to determine where the shortcomings put your business in a bind. Then put all your efforts into turning these drawbacks around to improve your results.

Take a hard look at yourself to give you direction for a realistic and objective approach for survival:

- Do away with personal needs and satisfaction

- Be very determined and anxious to move ahead

- Benefit from your knowledge

- Watch your progress closely

- Expect best results from yourself and others

- Don't be upset if things do not move as fast as you would like

- Gain by advice and look for new ideas

- Don't be deterred by setbacks

- Learn from your mistakes

- Be patient.

After going through tough times; benefit by the reasons that created this crucial period; how you pulled out; and how you can learn for the future. Use this past history of events as a learning experience which will be helpful not to cause similar incidents of set-backs in the subsequent years. Having gone through the traumatic crisis, you will have gained the knowledge and understanding of similar predicaments.

As you scan your background, it is amazing how some of the mistakes, oversights, and errors will help you develop new ideas and opportunities for your destined success.

Discover possible downfalls before they happen. There are warnings throughout your business life that alerts you to "pick up the ball and run." Study the caution signs; be prepared to counteract them, and don't ever lose control. Profit by your mistakes and move forward.

A very common downfall of a small business is to "temporarily" use payroll, unemployment, social security, or sales taxes as your own cash flow. Many times this dangerous habit can be the full reason that you cannot recoup your financial dilemma. Taking advantage of this "extra cash" they foolishly thought was available to them is a very serious blunder which can cost them their business -- by creating both legal and operational problems. This practice must cease and desist immediately.

A troubled company can gain quite a bit from their past if they are strong enough and alert to call for help to evaluate their problems. There are times in operating a business that you fail to see the "forest for the trees." It surely makes good business sense to retain for a short limited period an outside consultant to come in and give some advice and see things which obviously only a trained specialist can do. The cost will more than pay for itself.

Mistakes lead to improvement. Business is a constant learning process and capitalizing on difficulties and obstruction will lead to action which will put you on the track to rectify and develop. It will bring on innovations for another direction.

Utilize your flaws and past problems to inspire you and your organization to greater heights. Combine your association's drive and wisdom to create new thinking and a bigger challenge than ever before. Concentrate on the important ingredients of business which make it successful.

Every business from time to time is faced with reversed situations. These do not necessarily have to be a setback, but could stimulate your mind and action to reach a higher plateau. Too many people allow their problems to consume more energy than necessary, and tend to deter concentration in other areas which can be more important and productive.

Difficulties could act as an encouragement to push harder, profit from your mistakes, and act in a more positive position to correct. They will bring out the best in you and test your ingenuity to move forward.

A thorough study of each phase of your business, reviewing the shortcomings, capitalizing on the highlights, and openly discussing the good and the bad factors -- and above all doing something about it -- will bring you to higher heights than ever dreamed.

Leon Albin

Strategies that Worked in My Business

Everyone makes mistakes -- we made plenty.

I analyzed all facets and operations of our business to review with several people throughout our organization. We were open and frank to evaluate, and follow up for improvement anywhere we could. With each correction, we discussed how it would interact with what we were doing, commented about the progress it made, and benefitted from each occurrence.

We found corrective measures in every department. Firstly, we found that drop-shipping from the supplier directly to the stores whenever possible saved handling expenses as well as money to back up merchandise in our warehouse. It also meant better stock control; helped for less purchases; better turnover and improved working capital. This, of course, minimized the use of bank loans and less interest.

In our accounting department, we changed the payables to be more structured twice a month rather than on a daily basis. Further, our payroll changed from weekly to bi-weekly, cutting this expense of work. We made a study of register readings periodically during the day to slash the payroll.

In the area of purchasing, I increased departments and responsibilities to my buyers, eliminating one. Also, we shortened buying trips and accomplished the same results.

Everyone was made to realize that the less mistakes we duplicated, the more successful we would be.

Lessons Learned

- *Tear down and analyze your past for future improvement.*
- *Tough experiences can benefit development.*
- *Evaluate your key errors that lead to your problems.*
- *Study each phase of your business setbacks to avail change.*

CHAPTER 24

Face Failure With Optimism

Prelude

If all else failed in your efforts for survival, be ready "to pack your bag" and go on to the next endeavor. You can feel good about yourself that you have given it the "old college try". Stand proud that you have given all you can and use your background and experience to give you the optimism for your next opportunity.

Do not consider yourself a failure if your business does not survive. Harry Truman didn't make it as a habadasher -- but went on to be one of the outstanding presidents in the history of our country.

You must prepare yourself to face whatever life brings. If it was not meant for you to be in business, think of your alternatives. Facing the reality will give you a clear head to go to the next stage of your life. A setback in one field can open doors in another area -- or even in another business. But, the key is to stand up tall and move on.

The next game in town might present more of an opportunity than you have ever imagined. Don't look at a failure as the end. Think of it as the new beginning. This realistic attitude will not emphasize your demise -- but will open up to you many businesses or opportunities available to you.

Give deep thought as to the diverse fields that you know of -- or put together areas of interest that you have. It will be surprising even to yourself of where you will go from this point.

Be realistic with yourself; analyze your strong and weak characteristics; broaden your scope of endeavors; pick out where you will be comfortable; and feel and know that there is a place for you.

There is a life after your business career -- but one failure does not close the door for all future opportunities. So if you go into the battle of salvaging your business with a positive outlook, the outcome could be better than you might expect.

Remember, it is to everybody's interest and benefit to have your company survive. Retention of a faltering business is of importance to all, as everyone gains monetarily and personally. The creditors and banks will have more of their debts paid back; the suppliers will have the ability for future sales and distribution; and the employees will keep jobs to support their families.

Realizing all the above interested and affected parties, it puts you in the key position of staying intact. Knowing that there are a lot of people around you with a vested interest, you should feel good about having the opportunity to continue.

After performing the necessary and tactical steps for survival and doing all possible to continue your business, you have every right to feel that everything has been done and you must hope for the best and be optimistic as to what happens next. You would have no reason to look back about the past and think what else you could have done.

Face the future feeling good. If it didn't pull together, you must be convinced that all has been done. Stay optimistic and keep your mind open to think positive. But always be ready to face whatever happens -- so as to avail yourself in another direction.

Strategies that Worked in My Business

Everyone hopes for success, but those that are prepared to accept the worst are more capable of handling a serious crisis, if it happens.

I had readied and trained myself to tolerate any fate that would come my way. It gave me strength and made me steadfast to do my best while I aimed at eliminating stress during my trying days.

There were many times I didn't think I would make it through the month, but I always managed to lift myself and say, "You're going to make it." I felt self-assured that there were plenty of opportunities for me if I failed.

I encouraged myself to look to the future and felt confident that my years in business had given me the experience, fortitutde and marketability to enter into a similar field, or anything else I would choose. This belief in myself actually made me stronger to survive and make the turnaround I accomplished successful.

Lessons Learned

- *Failure can be the beginning of a new success.*
- *Work on your strengths and pursue opportunities in your most potent direction.*
- *Be optimistic for best results.*

CHAPTER 25

Set Up a Goal to Attain

Prelude

Whether you remain in business or go on to another venture, set a goal for you to conquer, and how you will get there. Be realistic and subjective and work to attain it.

When all is said and done, whether you remain in business, sell your business, or go out, you must set your sights where you want to go -- and the goal on how to get there. Each direction of endeavor must follow a plan. List your options to decide which path is best for you.

If you have decided that your game plan is to be in business, map out thoroughly how to get there. As discussed throughout this book, the improvement of operation, the change of merchandising, finding new markets, the up-lifting of personnel and the confidence and support of your creditors

Leon Albin

and suppliers all play an integral part of the entire formula to meet a target.

Think positive for the future. Concentrate on a brighter prospective of business progress. Don't neglect your everyday activities -- but surely you must put much effort into your advancement. Be confident and work for future success.

Set up your objective for planned improvement, reorganize, and be flexible as to adapting to future growth. Prepare your organization and employees to blend in to meet the new demands and challenges.

Your realistic goals will be attained if you follow your plans with a course of action. Results will happen if you have adequate funds, proper knowledge, good organization, the commitment, and the motivation to succeed.

A strong retention objective, utilizing governmental assistance programs for counselling, consulting, and workshops will help you achieve your aim of reversing poor management and accomplishing survival and turnaround.

They could work hand in hand identifying problems and plan implementation to find solutions. They could aid in strategizing to recognize temporary situations which can be positioned for future success to rebuild a healthy company. You must be prepared to instill an improved strategy; rectify poor operational efficiency; upgrade your overall procedures; and reform bad habits within your organization.

You have been through all the tests and have passed with flying colors. The theme at this time is positive thinking, a new lease on life, and raring to go for renewed profitable heights.

Make a thorough review as to the trying ordeal you have gone through and create new habits with corrective measures to attain new goals and heights. Organize your entire business from the unskilled employees to your top assistants. Confidence must be instilled in everyone, making them feel part of a newly revived organization that is going places. Set up meetings on a one-to-one basis and also departments to emphasize where you are going from this point. Compliment them on what they have done in the past; and the integral and significant part he or she plays in your future plans.

Your entire organization must feel important and must realize how much meaning each has in the re-building process. Explain any new organizational framework and particularly all the innovative changes.

People are most concerned about cutbacks and how it would affect them. The organization would watch closely how and where the expenses are reduced. The biggest impetus to change would be what the plans are for restructuring and seeking new management. It could be looked at favorably as well as for growth potential.

If your plan is to sell out -- then putting together the proper and enticing proposal is important to arrive at a practical price. A sound presentation to an interested buyer must be done as to highlight the focal points to develop a sale. The price must be in line with fair ratios of profit or loss in order to push the potential buyer to go forward with the deal. Everything has its price -- and being fair and practical will make the sale. Be sure to bring out the potential of the business and openly discuss its problems and solutions.

If you intend to continue in business, again spell out step by step what you propose to do. Don't shoot for the moon -- but be realistic and enthusiastic of your plans. Pull in the people around you who have any interest and clearly enlighten them as to your new organizational ideas. Sell them on your thoughts and welcome their participation and involvement to move ahead with you.

Try to get everyone who has worked with you in the past; and get as much new blood as possible to share your goal and determination for success. Above all, commitment is important to yourself, focus where you want to be and follow through.

The priority goal and the most important objective in remaining in business is to earn a profit. The net profit of a business is the net difference of income less expenses -- taking into consideration individual owner or partnership salaries. The bottom line of profit does not have to necessarily be in cash, but can include new assets of furniture, fixtures and merchandise.

Strategies that Worked in My Business

I have always been motivated and driven by a force of attainment and inspired by the feeling and confidence that I would reach my objective.

Throughout my years in business, I have set many aspirations to achieve. All my transitions from one type and format to another was put together with a definite pattern to follow. Things seemed to fall in place where they were expected to fit if I planned with deliberation. It doesn't map its own path.

Every one of my accomplishments was set by a procedure to make it happen. Each problem or project I was faced with in business needed an answer which required a scheme. Whether it was internal dealing with situations which I had control over, or outside suppliers or credtiors, there was always satisfaction when they were preceeded by the appropriate thoughts.

It took deep planning to accomplish the sale of my company in order to reap the best deal and one which would have a meeting of the minds. It was accomplished quickly and successfully because strong goals were set which were fair to all parties.

I generally found that the more thought put into a proposal, the better was the result.

Lessons Learned

- *Evaluate your direction to pursue.*
- *Study your options and organize your path.*
- *Review all phases of business operation to determine your sights ahead.*
- *Restructure your goal with strong objectives.*

CHAPTER 26

Reaping the Turnabout Results

Prelude

> *The joy of a turnaround will be shared with you by all the parties involved -- from employees to creditors. Everyone will be ready to move forward with better attitudes, renewed interest and confidence.*

After going through the experience of a business reversal, the road to recovery is a sweet path. Never forget the problems created by taking your guard off and the situation you went through because of the bad business climate you witnessed. It is not uncommon to take steps backward in order to be able to move forward.

You will now find the change-about of the surrounding "world" taking a better attitude and renewed interest in going ahead with you.

Employees' morale will jump and become enthusiastic about their jobs. The revitalization of your company will create more interest and morale for flourishment and continued success. They will want to know about future plans and how they will be involved.

Their concerns and confidence must be encouraged by you indicating to them your appreciation and cooperation. Extra benefits and incentives should be offered to keep their interest. It isn't necessary to invest large sums of monies -- but little things showing that you are thinking of them can accomplish this purpose. Consideration of adaptable schedules, flexibility with family needs, changed hours and further responsibilities are just a few ideas that work.

It is amazing how your creditors and financial people and other companies who have relations with you will adjust favorably with your resurgency. Your community, your customers and others who have dealings with you will all take note of you getting back on your feet.

Strategic planning for continuance of your road back to sound business must be organized with a deep obligation to maintain your objectives. Emphasize the company's strengths and possibilities. Play on your new products, markets and supplier resources.

Your proposal for the future must set out for your company where and how you intend to accomplish your goals.

Put heavy emphasis on responsibility and gain all the enjoyment of the results and efforts you worked so hard to achieve. Keep an air of confidence and enthusiasm and let it all rub off with everyone to share the good days ahead.

Your environment of suppliers, bankers, customers, employees, everyone who helped you back, and each person and company who will be involved in your revitalized business should be proud of your "new" organization.

Getting back on track and accomplishing a successful turnaround requires deep thought and plotting not only for present stability, but all avenues must be studied for future opportunities. Re-examine and evaluate your past operation and procedures. Profit from past mistakes and shortcomings by looking at your business with utmost confidence for survival and growth. Keep a handle on your day-to-day activities and beware of over-expansion.

Having accomplished a successful turnaround project, the rewards of a comeback will be very gratifying. It has been a touch and go wait, but you have arrived at the turning point -- going back up. Now your priority must be to run a successful business to achieve an annual net profit. It usually takes several years to produce real profitability. Constantly stay on the look-out for new ideas and innovations.

As the breakeven point is met (starting of profit) and after a stabilizing period, begin looking at expansion to move ahead. It is now the appropriate time to look over your operation for more efficiency, production and sales. Thoughts should be given to changing or incorporating certain phases to free up time for extension or improvement of other areas. It could be beneficial for the company to "farm out" key departments to free up employees' expertise to other departments.

Re-establishing a profit was generated by better operational habits and procedures, creating a higher cash flow and the ability to pay taxes.

The joy and happiness of all those who were connected in the participation of a successful turnaround is that each and every one benefits from the results, profits, and success with vision and hope for the future.

Strategies that Worked in My Business

The turnaround in my business resulted in the sale of my company, but any business can relate to success after going through the ordeals of survival.

The prime accomplishment was to put my organization back on solid grounds. Since that was achieved, the decision of continuation or a sell out was very gratifying. I chose to sell because of the unusual opportunity presented. However, a turnaround reaps satisfaction beyond imagination and the opportunity is extremely comforting.

When our employees felt the impact of success, they shared their enthusiasm. The comeback to them meant more secure jobs, or a chance with the new company. It didn't spell out the end, but a new beginning. Additional incentives were discussed and they seemed to feel possibilities for their future.

My suppliers were excited because either the continuation or selling out to a new company would maintain their sales and even beyond.

The doors are now open for future, imminent growth and everyone involved shared in the opportunities ahead.

Lessons Learned

- *Play on everyone who is interested and affected by your business with heir strong input.*
- *Organize your future with deep commitment.*

Leon Albin

- *Include your banker, creditors and your entire organizational team in your turnaround.*

- *Encourage their efforts and enthusiasm.*